An Analysis of

Henry David Thoreau's

Civil Disobedience

Mano Toth
with
Jason Xidias

Published by Macat International Ltd
24:13 Coda Centre, 189 Munster Road, London SW6 6AW.

Distributed exclusively by Routledge
2 Park Square, Milton Park, Abingdon, Oxon OX14 4RN
711 Third Avenue, New York, NY 10017, USA

Routledge is an imprint of the Taylor & Francis Group, an informa business

www.macat.com
info@macat.com

Cataloguing in Publication Data
A catalogue record for this book is available from the British Library.
Library of Congress Cataloguing-in-Publication Data is available upon request.
Cover illustration: Capucine Deslouis

ISBN 978-1-912303-48-9 (hardback)
ISBN 978-1-912127-05-4 (paperback)
ISBN 978-1-912282-36-4 (e-book)

Notice
The information in this book is designed to orientate readers of the work under analysis,
to elucidate and contextualise its key ideas and themes, and to aid in the development
of critical thinking skills. It is not meant to be used, nor should it be used, as a
substitute for original thinking or in place of original writing or research. References and
notes are provided for informational purposes and their presence does not constitute
endorsement of the information or opinions therein. This book is presented solely for
educational purposes. It is sold on the understanding that the publisher is not engaged
to provide any scholarly advice. The publisher has made every effort to ensure that
this book is accurate and up-to-date, but makes no warranties or representations with
regard to the completeness or reliability of the information it contains. The information
and the opinions provided herein are not guaranteed or warranted to produce particular
results and may not be suitable for students of every ability. The publisher shall not be
liable for any loss, damage or disruption arising from any errors or omissions, or from
the use of this book, including, but not limited to, special, incidental, consequential or
other damages caused, or alleged to have been caused, directly or indirectly, by the
information contained within.

CONTENTS

THE MACAT LIBRARY

The Macat Library is a series of unique academic explorations of seminal works in the humanities and social sciences – books and papers that have had a significant and widely recognised impact on their disciplines. It has been created to serve as much more than just a summary of what lies between the covers of a great book. It illuminates and explores the influences on, ideas of, and impact of that book. Our goal is to offer a learning resource that encourages critical thinking and fosters a better, deeper understanding of important ideas.

Each publication is divided into three Sections: Influences, Ideas, and Impact. Each Section has four Modules. These explore every important facet of the work, and the responses to it.

This Section-Module structure makes a Macat Library book easy to use, but it has another important feature. Because each Macat book is written to the same format, it is possible (and encouraged!) to cross-reference multiple Macat books along the same lines of inquiry or research. This allows the reader to open up interesting interdisciplinary pathways.

To further aid your reading, lists of glossary terms and people mentioned are included at the end of this book (these are indicated by an asterisk [*] throughout) – as well as a list of works cited.

Macat has worked with the University of Cambridge to identify the elements of critical thinking and understand the ways in which six different skills combine to enable effective thinking.
Three allow us to fully understand a problem; three more give us the tools to solve it. Together, these six skills make up the **PACIER** model of critical thinking. They are:

ANALYSIS – understanding how an argument is built
EVALUATION – exploring the strengths and weaknesses of an argument
INTERPRETATION – understanding issues of meaning

CREATIVE THINKING – coming up with new ideas and fresh connections
PROBLEM-SOLVING – producing strong solutions
REASONING – creating strong arguments

To find out more, visit **WWW.MACAT.COM.**

CRITICAL THINKING AND *CIVIL DISOBEDIENCE*

Primary critical thinking skill: CREATIVE THINKING
Secondary critical thinking skill: REASONING

In *Civil Disobedience*, Henry David Thoreau looks at old issues in new ways, asking: is there ever a time when individuals should actively oppose their government and its justice system?

After a thorough review of the evidence, Thoreau comes to the conclusion that opposition is legitimate whenever government actions or institutions are unacceptable to an individual's conscience. What is particularly interesting is that Thoreau's creative mind took him deeper into the argument, as he concluded that this legitimate opposition really wasn't enough. In Thoreau's opinion, anyone who believed something to be wrong had a duty to resist it actively.

These ideas were completely at odds with the prevailing opinions of the day – that it was the duty of every citizen to support the state. Thoreau connected ideas and notions in a novel manner and went against the tide, generating new hypotheses so that people could see matters in a new light. It is a mark of the success of his creative thinking that his views are now considered mainstream, and that his arguments are still deployed in defence of the principle of civil disobedience.

ABOUT THE AUTHOR OF THE ORIGINAL WORK

Henry David Thoreau was born in Concord, Massachusetts, in 1817 and lived there for almost his entire life. The town and the surrounding countryside made a profound impression on him, and he is as well known for his nature writing as for his political ideas. Thoreau went to Harvard College and afterwards became part of a group of thinkers—the Transcendentalists—who were convinced of the importance of nature, morality, and individual freedom. Thoreau's own writings did not reach a wide audience during his lifetime (he died in 1862, aged just 44), but they became much more important in the twentieth century.

ABOUT THE AUTHORS OF THE ANALYSIS

Mano Toth is researching for a PhD in politics at the University of Cambridge.

Dr Jason Xidias holds a PhD in European Politics from King's College London, where he completed a comparative dissertation on immigration and citizenship in Britain and France. He was also a Visiting Fellow in European Politics at the University of California, Berkeley. Currently, he is Lecturer in Political Science at New York University.

ABOUT MACAT

GREAT WORKS FOR CRITICAL THINKING

Macat is focused on making the ideas of the world's great thinkers accessible and comprehensible to everybody, everywhere, in ways that promote the development of enhanced critical thinking skills.

It works with leading academics from the world's top universities to produce new analyses that focus on the ideas and the impact of the most influential works ever written across a wide variety of academic disciplines. Each of the works that sit at the heart of its growing library is an enduring example of great thinking. But by setting them in context – and looking at the influences that shaped their authors, as well as the responses they provoked – Macat encourages readers to look at these classics and game-changers with fresh eyes. Readers learn to think, engage and challenge their ideas, rather than simply accepting them.

'Macat offers an amazing first-of-its-kind tool for interdisciplinary learning and research. Its focus on works that transformed their disciplines and its rigorous approach, drawing on the world's leading experts and educational institutions, opens up a world-class education to anyone.'

Andreas Schleicher
Director for Education and Skills, Organisation for Economic
Co-operation and Development

'Macat is taking on some of the major challenges in university education ... They have drawn together a strong team of active academics who are producing teaching materials that are novel in the breadth of their approach.'

Prof Lord Broers,
former Vice-Chancellor of the University of Cambridge

'The Macat vision is exceptionally exciting. It focuses upon new modes of learning which analyse and explain seminal texts which have profoundly influenced world thinking and so social and economic development. It promotes the kind of critical thinking which is essential for any society and economy.
This is the learning of the future.'

Rt Hon Charles Clarke, former UK Secretary of State for Education

'The Macat analyses provide immediate access to the critical conversation surrounding the books that have shaped their respective discipline, which will make them an invaluable resource to all of those, students and teachers, working in the field.'

Professor William Tronzo, University of California at San Diego

WAYS IN TO THE TEXT

KEY POINTS

- Henry David Thoreau is widely recognized as one of the most important writers in the tradition of North American literature. He is associated with self-reliance, nonconformity* (a rejection of certain kinds of social expectations and norms), and nonviolent resistance.

- In *Civil Disobedience* (1866), he argues that individuals have a moral duty to challenge governments if the policies or laws of those governments are unjust.

- Civil disobedience is an important concept in political philosophy and has served as the basis for many nonviolent struggles against injustice.

Who Was Henry David Thoreau?

Henry David Thoreau, the author of *Civil Disobedience,* was born in 1817 in Concord, Massachusetts—the site of the first armed struggle of the American Revolution* (the conflict in which the young United States successfully fought the forces of the British Empire for its independence). Thoreau loved the town and its beautiful natural setting, and he lived there most of his life. His father, a storekeeper and pencil-maker, was unsuccessful in business, and Thoreau suffered considerable financial hardship growing up. His mother was an active participant in the Concord Female Charitable Society,* a charity founded by local women.

Thoreau went to Harvard College* (now Harvard University) with the help of a scholarship and financial assistance from his extended family; he received a Bachelor of Arts degree in 1837. At Harvard, he came into contact with prominent intellectuals, notably the poet Ralph Waldo Emerson.*

After graduating from college, he became part of a group of intellectuals known as the Transcendentalists.* Based on the East Coast of the United States, the Transcendentalists wrote about the importance of nature, morality, and individual freedom, and the group included literary figures such as Emerson, the anti-slavery activist Theodore Parker,* the writer Elizabeth Peabody,* and the early feminist Margaret Fuller.*

In 1846, Thoreau spent a night in prison for refusing to pay a tax required if one was to vote, known as poll tax,* as a protest against slavery in the United States and against the Mexican–American War* of 1846–8 (a conflict that followed the United State's annexation of the territory of Texas). This brief experience shaped his outlook on social resistance and became an important theme in his later writings.

The author died in 1862 at the age of 44. *Civil Disobedience* was his most influential work. Although his writings received very little attention during his lifetime, Thoreau has been widely recognized as one of America's most important writers since his death. Today, he is usually associated with self-reliance, nonconformity, and nonviolent resistance.

What Does *Civil Disobedience* Say?

On January 26, 1848, Thoreau gave a lecture, "The Rights and Duties of the Individual in Relation to Government," and delivered it again three weeks later. In May 1849, he published an essay based on those lectures, "Resistance to Civil Government." Thoreau's sister Sophia Thoreau* and his friend the poet Ellery Channing* edited that lecture after his death, and it appeared in an 1866 anthology of essays, *A Yankee in Canada, with Anti-slavery and Reform Papers*.[1] Although the text contained only minor changes, it acquired a new title: *Civil Disobedience*.

Civil Disobedience presents a critique of American government, which, in Thoreau's view, "never of itself furthered any enterprise."[2] All that the country had accomplished, the author writes, was due to the "character inherent in the American people," and, "if the government had not sometimes got in its way,"[3] much more could have been achieved.

More generally, Thoreau claims in the essay, "Government is at best but an expedient"; its power is "liable to be abused and perverted." Essentially, in his view, the motto "that government is best which governs least" could be better expressed as "that government is best which governs not at all."[4] He goes on to attack specific actions and institutions of the American state on moral grounds, in particular the Mexican–American War and slavery.

He also argues in *Civil Disobedience* that the possibility of injustice is deeply ingrained in the founding principles of the United States. He challenges the idea of majority rule,* claiming that nothing is inherently good in the will of the majority. The reason why the majority is allowed to rule is merely practical; it is "not because they are the most likely to be in the right, nor because this seems fairest to the minority, but because they are physically the strongest."[5]

Thoreau criticizes the rule of law—or, more precisely, the uncritical acceptance of and docile obedience to rules. He believes that "law never made men a whit more just; and, by means of their respect for it, even the well-disposed are daily made the agents of injustice."[6]

The book's main and most influential argument centers on the dilemma of the individual who strives to be a moral person while being subjected to the power of the state. Thoreau argues that we should each answer to our consciences first and place our duties as citizens second; a person's conscience should always overrule the state's demands on the citizen. So, according to him, when citizenship and conscience are in conflict and the state requires something different from an individual's own conscience, when injustice "is of such a nature that it requires you to be an agent of injustice to another, then, I say, break the law."[7] This is the essence of civil disobedience. When this conflict between state and conscience becomes acute, Thoreau claims "resistance to civil government" is not only legitimate but also a moral imperative.

Why Does *Civil Disobedience* Matter?

Thoreau addresses the social issues of his time; his ideas about politics and the individual's duty to the state work on a more general level. The founding principles of the American political system—namely, majority rule and the rule of law—have become more relevant as democratic governments have taken root in more countries. And Thoreau sets out a timeless and universal central problem: the dilemma of the individual who must choose between obeying his or her conscience or obeying his or her government.

The most original feature of the text is that, in contrast to other political thinkers, Thoreau turns on its head the main question of political obligation: "Why is the individual duty-bound to obey the government?" Instead, he asks: "When does the individual have a duty to *disobey* political authority?"

Thoreau makes a strong moral claim by connecting this question with conscience and social injustices. While he doesn't advocate the abolition of government altogether, his view stands in stark contrast to the dominant moral theories of his day. It was an original contribution to a long-running question in political philosophy—one that everyone from the ancient Greek philosopher Aristotle* to the British philosophers Thomas Hobbes* and John Locke* had addressed.

Civil Disobedience would eventually make a major impact. This was due partly to the way Thoreau merged a general political critique with particular issues of the day. It also resulted from the fact that Thoreau practiced what he preached. Addressing the major social issues of the day, as well as personally behaving according to the moral theory he developed, gave weight to his argument. The work does, nevertheless, contain many ambiguities, and Thoreau's lack of clarity is one reason why his concept is so widespread today—it can be interpreted in many different ways.

Today, the concept of civil disobedience is an important idea in political philosophy. Even beyond academic circles, the text has inspired many thinkers and resistance movements. Thoreau's name may not always be mentioned in connection with these movements, but his views on morality and the individual's obligation to engage in nonviolent resistance continue to make an impact on social developments and contemporary scholarly debates.

NOTES

1 The title "Civil Disobedience," by which the work is popularly known, was first used for an edited version of the text that appeared in 1866, after the author's death. The edition used in this analysis is the very first publication of the essay: Henry David Thoreau, "Resistance to Civil Government," in *Aesthetic Papers*, ed. Elizabeth Palmer Peabody (Boston: The Editor, 1849). However, another version can be found in Henry David Thoreau, "Civil Disobedience," in *A Yankee in Canada, with Anti-slavery and Reform Papers*, eds. Sophia E. Thoreau and William Ellery Channing (Boston: Ticknor & Fields, 1866), 123–51. This text uses the *Aesthetic Papers* copy.

2 Thoreau, "Resistance to Civil Government," 189.

3 Thoreau, "Resistance to Civil Government," 190.

4 Thoreau, "Resistance to Civil Government," 189.

5 Thoreau, "Resistance to Civil Government," 190.

6 Thoreau, "Resistance to Civil Government," 190–1.

7 Thoreau, "Resistance to Civil Government," 198.

SECTION 1
INFLUENCES

MODULE 1
THE AUTHOR AND THE
HISTORICAL CONTEXT

KEY POINTS

- *Civil Disobedience* makes the case for morality, self-reliance, nonconformity,* and nonviolent resistance to political authority. These are important concepts in political philosophy and have served as the basis for social struggles.

- When Thoreau made a protest against slavery in the United States by refusing to pay a poll tax* (a tax imposed on all those who wished to vote), he was sent to prison overnight. That experience shaped his ideas about the importance of moral duty over law.

- Slavery and the Mexican–American War* of 1846 to 1848 — a conflict that provoked debate on slavery in the United States — molded Thoreau's views on social justice and moral obligation.

Why Read This Text?

Civil Disobedience (1849), one of Henry David Thoreau's rare political texts, asks whether a nation's citizens sometimes have a moral duty to disobey its laws. In it, Thoreau combines a critique of the politics of his day with a general theoretical challenge to ideas of political obligation that were common at the time. His conclusion is that resistance to civil government may not only be permissible but also is the only morally defensible option in some circumstances.

Thoreau's argument is that every conscientious citizen has a moral duty to oppose and even break unjust laws, refusing allegiance to a state that requires the individual to become an "agent of injustice." His

> ❝ Must the citizen ever for a moment, or in the least degree, resign his conscience, then? I think that we should be men first, and subjects afterward. ❞
>
> Henry David Thoreau, *Civil Disobedience*

essay received little attention at the time of its publication, but it was a challenge to existing theories of government and allegiance, and it established an alternative approach that has become highly influential and increasingly relevant over time in academic circles and beyond.

Thoreau's ideas fit within the movement known as Transcendentalism*—a way of thinking and living that valued nature and simplicity, placing morality above materialism. These ideas would become widely accepted partly because he never called for the abolition of government altogether as a means of overcoming injustice. Since the publication of *Civil Disobedience*, Thoreau's core concepts— moral obligation, nonconformity, and nonviolent resistance—have formed the basis of social struggles around the world.

Author's Life

Thoreau was born in 1817 in Concord, Massachusetts. After graduating from Harvard College* (now Harvard University) in 1837, he returned to his hometown and lived there until his death in 1862. He loved hiking and being in the countryside, and though his political essays have been highly influential,[1] he is actually best known for his nature writings[2] and the narratives he wrote about his excursions.[3] In 1846, he went to jail for a night because he had refused to pay the poll tax for six years as a stand against slavery in the United States and the Mexican–American War* (1846–8). That experience helped to formulate his thoughts on civil resistance; he used the story of his imprisonment in his later essays.

Thoreau published several works, but *Civil Disobedience* was his most influential political piece, one based on his life experiences. Thoreau lived his entire life in Massachusetts, which, in 1780, was one of the first American states to abolish slavery. Over time, most of the northern territories followed suit, but many slave-owners in the South had strong economic reasons to preserve the practice. During the first half of the nineteenth century, it became an increasingly controversial issue as the movement to abolish slavery gained support.

Author's Background

In the text, Thoreau makes clear that, in addition to his overnight experience in a Massachusetts prison, two contemporary political issues greatly influenced his ideas about resistance to civil government: the institution of slavery and the country's war with Mexico.

In the first half of the nineteenth century, the United States was rapidly expanding its territory westwards. Thoreau objected to the war and saw the nation's invasion of Mexico as a means simply to acquire new land. His home state of Massachusetts had abolished slavery in 1780, but the question of slavery had become a source of increasing social tension throughout America. The southern states allowed the use of slave labor, while the northern territories generally prohibited it.

Thoreau was a passionate abolitionist*—that is, someone opposed to the institution of slavery—and he thought that those who claimed they opposed slavery were not doing enough to end it. He saw it as an unacceptable, unjust practice. Shortly before his death, tensions over this issue erupted into the American Civil War,* a conflict fought between the northern states that opposed the practice, and the southern states that wished it to continue. After the victory of the North, slavery was abolished throughout the United States.

Both of these issues strengthened Thoreau's belief that morality and justice were more important than material concerns—that is, the economic benefits of slavery or new lands and, in the latter case, the desire to gain control of such places as Texas, California, and New Mexico before Britain did.

NOTES

1   Henry David Thoreau, "Resistance to Civil Government," in *Aesthetic Papers*, ed. Elizabeth Palmer Peabody (Boston: The Editor, 1849); "A Plea for Captain John Brown," in *Echoes of Harper's Ferry*, ed. James Redpath (Boston: Thayer & Eldridge, 1860), 17–42.

2   Henry David Thoreau, *A Week on the Concord and Merrimack Rivers* (Boston: James Munroe & Co., 1849); *Walden* (Boston: Ticknor & Fields, 1854).

3   Henry David Thoreau, *Excursions* (Boston: Ticknor & Fields, 1863); *The Maine Woods*, eds. Sophia E. Thoreau and William Ellery Channing (Boston: Ticknor & Fields, 1864); *Cape Cod*, eds. Sophia E. Thoreau and William Ellery Channing (Boston: Ticknor & Fields, 1865); *A Yankee in Canada, with Anti-slavery and Reform Papers*, eds. Sophia E. Thoreau and William Ellery Channing (Boston: Ticknor & Fields, 1866).

MODULE 2
ACADEMIC CONTEXT

KEY POINTS

- Thoreau wrote *Civil Disobedience* in 1849 against the historical backdrop of slavery* in the United States and the Mexican–American War*—a conflict fought between the United States and Mexico that served to highlight issues concerning slavery.

- He was a prominent member of the Transcendentalist movement,* which emphasized the importance of morality over materialism. The poet Ralph Waldo Emerson,* also a Transcendentalist, was Thoreau's mentor and most important intellectual influence.

- Thoreau believed that slavery and American imperialism,* the nation's policy of empire building, were unjust. He argued, as part of the wider abolitionist* movement, that individuals had a right and a moral obligation to challenge harmful policies and laws.

The Work in its Context

Henry David Thoreau was a distinguished member of the Transcendentalist movement,* a school of thought that was prominent in American cultural life in the 1830s and 1840s and that clearly influenced *Civil Disobedience*. The poet Ralph Waldo Emerson,* the intellectual leader of the movement and a close friend, helped shape Thoreau's ideas. The Transcendentalists saw both nature and the individual as inherently good and disapproved of many social developments that they thought endangered this natural purity. Some Transcendentalist ideas—such as the belief in the independence of the

> ❝ Talk about slavery! It is not the peculiar institution of the South. It exists wherever men are bought and sold, wherever a man allows himself to be made a mere thing or a tool, and surrenders his inalienable rights of reason and conscience. ❞
>
> Henry David Thoreau, *Walden*

individual and a good conscience as the true source for judging right from wrong—appear as underlying assumptions in *Civil Disobedience*.

Thoreau's greatest contribution to this intellectual tradition is *Walden* (1854), an account of the 26 months he spent in a cabin he built near Walden Pond. It is a reflection on living simply in nature, and it stresses the importance of individualism, independence, self-reliance, self-sufficiency, and discovering oneself through spirituality.

Overall, *Civil Disobedience* is a product of the cultural and intellectual environment in which Thoreau lived. The author links his Transcendentalist ideas with important contemporary political developments, such as slavery and American imperialist action in Mexico. Ultimately, he was determined to challenge injustice, "cost what it may."[1]

Overview of the Field

The great public debates of contemporary America influenced Thoreau in his writing of *Civil Disobedience*. Abolitionism* was gathering strength in the first half of the nineteenth century. With *Civil Disobedience*, Thoreau added his voice to this debate.

The novelty of his approach was that he did not attack the slave owners in the South, but mostly addressed his fellow citizens in Massachusetts. "I quarrel not with far-off foes," he says in the text, "but with those who, near at home, co-operate with, and do the bidding of, those far away, and without whom the latter would be harmless."[2] He urges those who say they oppose slavery but who do "nothing in earnest and with effect" to be consistent and to take action against injustice.[3]

He argues in *Civil Disobedience* that conscientious individuals should actively withdraw their support from a state that compels them to be, directly or indirectly, part of grave injustices. Apart from slavery, Thoreau was also outraged by America's imperialist tendencies. In the essay, he explicitly speaks out against American actions in the Mexican–American War (1846–8).

Thoreau consistently practiced the civil disobedience* that he preached. He thought that refusing to pay taxes was an effective protest against the state and its unjust practices of slavery and war. Because he had refused to pay his poll tax,* he was imprisoned for a night in 1846. His experiences in jail were fundamentally important for crystallizing his views on civil resistance and the "half-witted" state.[4] This prison theme would become an integral part of *Civil Disobedience* and his later work.

Academic Influences

Ralph Waldo Emerson was the most important intellectual influence on Thoreau. He was a minister, poet, and philosopher, and is widely recognized as the father of Transcendentalism. In 1837, Emerson gave a lecture, "The American Scholar," at Harvard College. Thoreau was in the audience and profoundly moved by the talk. A friendship grew between the two men and, in 1841, Thoreau moved into Emerson's home, earning his keep as a handyman and by taking care of Emerson's children.

They were both members of the Transcendental Club, a group of New England intellectuals that also included the teacher Amos Bronson Alcott* and the editor Margaret Fuller.* Emerson took on the role of Thoreau's mentor and instilled in him an appreciation for individualism, simplicity, self-reliance, freedom of thought, and moral obligation. In particular, Emerson argued that conformity corrupted self-reflection and morality. He believed that no matter what society said or did, it was your obligation to do what you truly believed was correct, regardless of the consequences. Thoreau, in his work, followed a similar line of thought, arguing that individuals had the moral obligation to oppose government policies and laws that were unjust, particularly in the case of slavery.

NOTES

1   Henry David Thoreau, "Resistance to Civil Government," in *Aesthetic Papers*, ed. Elizabeth Palmer Peabody (Boston: The Editor, 1849), 193.

2   Thoreau, "Resistance to Civil Government," 193.

3   Thoreau, "Resistance to Civil Government," 193–4.

4   Thoreau, "Resistance to Civil Government," 203.

MODULE 3
THE PROBLEM

KEY POINTS

- Thoreau contributed to a long-standing and evolving debate about the relationship between the individual and political authority. He did this by focusing on two principal social injustices: slavery* and the Mexican–American War.*

- Thoreau challenged the accepted view as advocated by the English thinker William Paley.* Paley argued that, if society would not benefit overall from challenging or trying to change political authority, every individual had a duty to submit to that authority.

- Thoreau took issue with this viewpoint, even going so far as to suggest that when the injustice is great, violence may sometimes be morally permissible.

Core Question

The core question Henry David Thoreau seeks to answer in *Civil Disobedience* (1849) is, "What should the conscientious individual do when the prevailing political power compels him or her, directly or indirectly, to support unjust social practices?" This question is part of a broader theoretical problem in political philosophy that explores the relationship between the individual and authority. More specifically, it is related to the impasse that has always haunted the development of consent theory:* if a legitimate government relies on the consent of the governed in theory, should this mean that a subject has the right to withdraw its consent from the government in practice?

Thoreau's question had, in one form or another, occupied the thoughts of other political theorists before him. He thought the

> 66 Is it not possible to take a step further towards recognizing and organizing the rights of man? There will never be a really free and enlightened State, until the State comes to recognize the individual as a higher and independent power, from which all its own power and authority are derived, and treats him accordingly. 99
>
> Henry David Thoreau, *Civil Disobedience*

question worth asking for two reasons.

First, he felt it was particularly relevant in the political context of the day. He identified two injustices that he believed his fellow citizens should oppose more vigorously: the institution of slavery and the Mexican–American War. Thoreau was searching for the morally right course of action when a government requires an individual to be implicated, directly or indirectly, in unjust practices.

Second, Thoreau believed that previous political theorists had failed to answer his question. Specifically, he criticized the English clergyman and philosopher William Paley's view that, if the effort to change society through acts of resistance caused more costs than benefits, it was better simply to submit to authority for the good of the many. Despite Thoreau's questioning of governmental power and people's obligations to submit to that power, however, he generally kept his distance from anarchist* trends of thought that rejected all forms of political authority.

The Participants

Thoreau asked essentially the same questions that William Paley did: Does the individual have a duty to obey authority? When can resistance to civil government be legitimate? However, Thoreau's approach and his answers differed significantly from Paley's. Instead of basing his argument as Paley did on utilitarian* assumptions (the idea that a "right" action is an action that causes the greatest happiness for the greatest number of people), he used some of the core assumptions of the Transcendentalist* movement. That intellectual movement held beliefs favoring the independence of the individual and the inherently good nature of an individual's conscience. In this way, Thoreau arrived at conclusions that were markedly different from Paley's answers.

Paley, an English philosopher of the eighteenth century, was considered by many to be a leading authority on moral issues. His book, *The Principles of Moral and Political Philosophy*, originally published in 1785, remained highly influential throughout much of the nineteenth century.[1] In the chapter, "The Duty of Submission to Civil Government Explained," Paley writes that such a duty is essentially a question of expediency. According to Paley, if resistance to power and efforts to change political arrangements do not bring overall benefits for the whole of society, every individual has a duty to submit to that power. He writes, "So long as the interest of the whole society requires it, that is, so long as the established government cannot be resisted or changed without public inconveniency, it is the will of God … that the established government be obeyed."[2]

Thoreau strongly disagreed. He did not believe that resistance to authority could be reduced to a cold-blooded calculation of maximum public convenience. In *Civil Disobedience* he says, "Paley appears never to have contemplated those cases to which the rule of expediency does not apply, in which a people, as well as an individual, must do justice, cost what it may."[3] Thoreau goes as far as claiming that sometimes injustice can be so great that even violence is morally permissible, arguing, "But even suppose blood should flow. Is there not a sort of bloodshed when the conscience is wounded? Through this wound a man's real manhood and immortality flow out, and he bleeds to an everlasting death."[4]

The Contemporary Debate

Slavery and the Mexican–American War were prominent topics of debate at the time of *Civil Disobedience's* publication. In the northern states, the abolitionists'* opposition to slavery was growing. Still booming in the South, slavery had already been banned in the North, including in Thoreau's home state of Massachusetts.

Thoreau felt that many people who claimed to be abolitionists were not doing enough to end slavery in practice. His most vehement criticism was directed toward those who objected to particular measures but who did "nothing in earnest and with effect."[5] He goes as far as to claim in the book, "Those who, while they disapprove of the character and measures of a government, yield to it their allegiance and support, are undoubtedly its most conscientious supporters, and so frequently the most serious obstacles to reform."[6] He says that people who say they oppose an injustice as grave as slavery should actively resist and withhold support from the government, whatever the consequences.

Meanwhile, the Mexican–American War of 1846–8 had originated as a dispute over who controlled Texas and where the southern border of the United States ended. The American government wanted sovereignty over California and New Mexico because, within the broader scope of its doctrine of westward expansion, they were key frontier locations. Government officials feared that if the nation did not take control of these territories immediately, Britain, its main rival, would do so. This war greatly expanded the overall territory of the United States and its economic power. Thoreau denounced it as an act of American imperialism,* or empire building.

NOTES

1   William Paley, *The Principles of Moral and Political Philosophy* (London: R. Faulder, 1785).

2   Paley, *Principles of Moral and Political Philosophy*, 64.

3   Henry David Thoreau, "Resistance to Civil Government," in *Aesthetic Papers*, ed. Elizabeth Palmer Peabody (Boston: The Editor, 1849), 193.

4   Thoreau, "Resistance to Civil Government," 200.

5   Thoreau, "Resistance to Civil Government," 194.

6   Thoreau, "Resistance to Civil Government," 196.

MODULE 4
THE AUTHOR'S CONTRIBUTION

KEY POINTS

- Thoreau argues that people should refuse to give their allegiance to any political system that requires them to be part of grave injustices.

- This argument contributed to the emerging school of thought known as Transcendentalism* and challenged the dominant view of utilitarianism* (the idea that the correct action is the one that ensures the greatest happiness for the greatest number of people).

- The author's argument was original because he fused existing Transcendentalist ideas with contemporary injustices—notably slavery* and the Mexican–American War*—arguing that people had a moral obligation to oppose a government that supported them.

Author's Aims

Henry David Thoreau's main reason for writing *Civil Disobedience* in 1849 was his abhorrence of slavery and American imperialist* tendencies toward Mexico. In the text, he expresses particular frustration with the inactivity of those claiming to oppose those two concerns who nevertheless "hesitate, and they regret, and sometimes they petition; but they do nothing in earnest and with effect."[1] So, his primary intentions were both to challenge those injustices and to make people realize that, by obeying the government, they were indirectly contributing to them. The only way slavery and war could be effectively challenged and the only morally defensible option for a conscientious individual, Thoreau believed, was to withdraw support

> ❝ It is not a man's duty, as a matter of course, to devote himself to the eradication of any, even the most enormous wrong; he may still properly have other concerns to engage him; but it is his duty, at least, to wash his hands of it, and, if he gives it no thought longer, not to give it practically his support. ❞
>
> Henry David Thoreau, *Civil Disobedience*

from the government. His aim was to encourage people to act according to their conscience because "action from principle ... changes things and relations."[2]

Thoreau argues that people should actively withdraw their allegiance from a political system that requires them to be part of any grave injustices it supports. The individual must resist—even if such defiance leads to violence and the consequences of defying power cannot be seen as more harmful than the injustices themselves.

Approach

Thoreau arrives at his belief in resistance to civil government by first broadly defining government itself in *Civil Disobedience*. He challenges political authority, stating his misgivings about slavery and the Mexican–American War, and also about some of the founding principles of the American political system itself, notably the rule of law and majority rule* (the principle that law should be made according to the wishes of a majority of a nation's citizens). He moves on to claim that, in cases of grave injustice, the individual must not only object to such injustices but must also withdraw support from the political system. He gives the example of refusing to pay taxes as one of the ways to accomplish that.

The ideas described in *Civil Disobedience* did not appear in

Thoreau's earlier works, which were not concerned with political issues. As a prominent member of the Transcendentalist movement,* he borrowed some of the fundamental assumptions of other members, notably the poet Ralph Waldo Emerson,* and those assumptions inform all his work. Two basic tenets that appear in *Civil Disobedience* are: 1) the independence and autonomy of the individual, and 2) the inherently good nature of the human conscience.

Although Thoreau could not be considered an anarchist*—that is, someone opposed to any form of government at all—his association with this intellectual movement, which does not accept any form of political authority, is far from clear. At one point, "unlike those who call themselves no-government men," he asks for "not at once no government, but *at once* a better government."[3] This suggests that he is calling for improvements in political authority rather than rejecting that authority altogether. Another passage, however, might imply that, in his view, the ideal conclusion of these improvements is no government: "That government is best which governs not at all; and when men are prepared for it, that will be the kind of government which they will have."[4]

Contribution in Context

Thoreau presents an original approach to the notion of resistance, an idea discussed by many political theorists before the publication of *Civil Disobedience*. A political philosophical text in the Transcendentalist tradition, the work opposes the dominant utilitarian* moral theory of the English thinker William Paley,* who answered similar questions to those asked by Thoreau in very different ways. Thoreau bases his argument on philosophical ideas that differ substantially from those of Paley. Both men disagree with the advocates of anarchism. Unlike "no-government men,"[5] Thoreau does not reject all forms of government, calling instead for improvements to create a "really free and enlightened State."[6]

Finally, Thoreau makes it clear that he is not arguing for a general, epic struggle against all forms of injustice. This distinguishes him from the duty to promote Christian beliefs that was (and indeed still is) important to those doing missionary* work—that is, to those deliberately working to convert unbelievers to the faith. Rather, he is arguing that morality must take precedence over materialism, and if one is against such injustices as slavery and the Mexican–American War, one must oppose the political authority that supports them by any means possible.

NOTES

1   Henry David Thoreau, "Resistance to Civil Government," in *Aesthetic Papers*, ed. Elizabeth Palmer Peabody (Boston: The Editor, 1849), 193–4.

2   Thoreau, "Resistance to Civil Government," 197.

3   Thoreau, "Resistance to Civil Government," 190.

4   Thoreau, "Resistance to Civil Government," 189.

5   Thoreau, "Resistance to Civil Government," 190.

6   Thoreau, "Resistance to Civil Government," 211.

SECTION 2
IDEAS

MODULE 5
MAIN IDEAS

KEY POINTS

- *Civil Disobedience* presents four main themes: 1) a broad critique of government, 2) the ways in which a conscientious individual should respond to unjust political authority, 3) the consequences of resistance, and 4) the ways in which government can be improved.

- Thoreau's main idea is that an individual must morally resist unjust political authority, whatever the consequences may be.

- He presents this core concept in a free-flowing narrative that lacks a clear structure.

Key Themes

Henry David Thoreau's *Civil Disobedience* (1849) lacks a clear structure and has no sections or headings to guide the reader.[1] Despite the flowing nature of the text and frequent detours in the main argument, however, four main themes can be identified.

The first is a critique of government. Specifically, Thoreau criticizes certain actions of the American government and particular institutions, such as slavery. More generally, he highlights the potential for grave injustices inherent in the idea of majority rule* (that is, that the will of the majority should be reflected in the passing of laws and social policy, for example) and uncritical acceptance and respect for the law.

The second theme builds on the first, considering how a conscientious individual should act. According to Thoreau, "We should be men first, and subjects afterward."[2] This means that keeping individual moral integrity should always take priority over a government's expectations of its citizens. If your government's

> ❝ If the injustice is part of the necessary friction of the machine of government, let it go, let it go: perchance it will wear smooth, certainly the machine will wear out. If the injustice has a spring, or a pulley, or a rope, or a crank, exclusively for itself, then perhaps you may consider whether the remedy will not be worse than the evil; but if it is of such a nature that it requires you to be the agent of injustice to another, then, I say, break the law. ❞
>
> Henry David Thoreau, *Civil Disobedience*

injustices are sufficiently grave, you must resist—even if it means withdrawing your allegiance to the state.

The third theme centers on the question of where this resistance might lead; Thoreau's answer is to "that separate, but more free and honorable ground, where the State places those who are not *with* her but *against* her"—in prison.[3] After discussing potential political injustices and the stance the individual must take toward them, Thoreau explains his own experiences of defying the state and his consequent imprisonment. In this way, he demonstrates that the consequences of resistance to civil government are not as terrifying as they might appear.

In the fourth theme, he gives his views concerning the creation of a better and more just government.

Exploring the Ideas

Thoreau begins his discussion with a critical examination of the American government. He attacks the institution of slavery as an economically motivated practice and the Mexican–American War* as an example of imperialism* that he cannot support. He also criticizes the system of law upon which America was founded and explains why he is against the principle of majority rule in particular.

In the second and most influential part of the essay, he reflects on the point at which the injustice ingrained in political authority becomes so grave that the moral person must take action. Thoreau claims that sometimes the individual must not only oppose the actions of a government but also refuse to support the political system itself. A possible consequence of actively defying the government is punishment.

He then focuses on his experience in prison for refusing to pay a poll tax*—a tax levied on anyone wishing to vote—as a protest against slavery. He explains that this did not deter him from disobeying authority, and promotes the refusal to pay taxes as a viable means of challenging unjust political authority. Throughout the text, he expresses a loosely connected set of ideas about what he would consider a "really free and enlightened State."[4] He does not formulate a comprehensive theory of a just political system, but he does declare that, contrary to anarchist* thinkers, he does not refuse all forms of political authority.

Language and Expression

Thoreau is consistent; his ideas form a coherent whole. And despite the unstructured way that he presents his argument and occasional ambiguities, there is a reasonably clear logical structure behind his reasoning.

Some of the mostly implicit assumptions on which Thoreau built his theory of civil disobedience, however, are not always quite so clear. First and foremost, Thoreau takes it for granted that an individual can be independent and autonomous, and that he or she can exist outside the influence of political authority; indeed, at our best, he argues, we always are and do. Thoreau, who borrowed these ideas from the Transcendentalists,* gives very few justifications and explanations for them, leaving them open to challenge.

A critic from a Foucauldian* theoretical background, for instance—that is, someone who subscribes to the theories of the twentieth-century French social theorist and historian Michel Foucault*—would see this model of power, in which power is understood as a substance that can be centrally organized and possessed, as fundamentally misconceived. Foucauldians believe power is decentralized and present in all parts of the social body. Therefore, the "individual is not ... power's opposite member; the individual is one of power's first effects."[5] Far from being independent and autonomous, the individual is a product of power and plays an active role in reproducing power, according to Michel Foucault and his followers. The individual cannot exist outside power.

NOTES

1 Henry David Thoreau, "Resistance to Civil Government," in *Aesthetic Papers*, ed. Elizabeth Palmer Peabody (Boston: The Editor, 1849), 189–213.

2 Thoreau, "Resistance to Civil Government," 190.

3 Thoreau, "Resistance to Civil Government," 200.

4 Thoreau, "Resistance to Civil Government," 211.

5 Michel Foucault, *Society Must Be Defended*, trans. David Macey (New York: Picador, 2003), 30.

MODULE 6
SECONDARY IDEAS

KEY POINTS

- The most important secondary idea in *Civil Disobedience* is that although resistance to political authority will probably entail legal consequences, this is the price of following one's moral conscience and obligation.

- The concept of civil disobedience* is a key theme in political philosophy, and it has served as the basis for many global struggles.

- Thoreau encourages people to challenge political authority. But, in contrast to anarchists,* he does not believe in abolishing the state altogether (although his view on this is ambiguous).

Other Ideas

In *Civil Disobedience* (1849), Henry David Thoreau criticizes the very foundation and principles of American government. Progressing to his main argument, he declares that the individual must withdraw support of a state in which injustices become too great to bear. According to Thoreau, everyone must answer to his or her own conscience first, while the duty to comply with the expectations of political authority comes second.

A theme of secondary importance follows from this assertion. If in cases of grave injustice the individual must resist at any cost, then he or she must also bear the consequences—punishment or even imprisonment. Thoreau uses his own experience of jail to illustrate the logical consequences of civil disobedience—harassment from the state and possible incarceration. Such consequences are not, however, as

> ❝ I could not help being struck with the foolishness of that institution which treated me as if I were mere flesh and blood and bones, to be locked up … I saw that, if there was a wall of stone between me and my townsmen, there was a still more difficult one to climb or break through, before they could get to be as free as I was. I did not for a moment feel confined, and the walls seemed a great waste of stone and mortar. ❞
> Henry David Thoreau, *Civil Disobedience*

terrifying as they may appear, says Thoreau. In any case, they should be seen as the price for following one's moral conscience and obligation to resist unjust political authority. In short, fear of the consequences must not prevent an individual from challenging the system.

Exploring the Ideas

In arguing that prison is sometimes the only morally defensible option, Thoreau says:"Under a government which imprisons any unjustly, the true place for a just man is also a prison … the only house in a slave-state in which a free man can abide with honor."[1] For Thoreau, physical punishment was a novel and liberating experience. He "did not for a moment feel confined, and the walls seemed a great waste of stone and mortar."[2] He realized that because he retained his moral integrity even in the face of punishment, he was freer than any of his fellow townsmen who had paid the tax. Ironically, he was released the following day not because he decided to obey the law, but because someone else, possibly his aunt, had paid the tax, which Thoreau felt was "unfortunate."[3]

Thoreau also gives numerous hints about his idea of a just political system, though he fails to develop anything close to a comprehensive theory. He calls for taking "a step further towards recognizing and organizing the rights of man."[4] He describes the "really free and enlightened State" as the one that "comes to recognize the individual as a higher and independent power, from which all its own power and authority are derived, and treats him accordingly."[5]

Although this prescription is neither very precise nor particularly revolutionary, it makes it clear that Thoreau does not deny all authority and so distances himself from anarchist thinkers and movements. Even though he is determined to "quietly declare war with the State,"[6] he makes it obvious from the beginning that he does not ask for "at once no government, but *at once* a better government."[7]

Overlooked

Thoreau believed that when the injustice caused by a government's actions becomes too great to bear, conscientious subjects must withdraw their support. That stood in sharp contrast to the dominant utilitarian* notions of the time, which asserted that the refusal to submit to political power cannot be legitimate if the social harm such defiance causes is greater than the good it tries to achieve.

In *Civil Disobedience,* Thoreau dismisses this rule of expediency on the grounds that the duties to one's conscience must always come before the duties to one's state ("we should be men first, and subjects afterward")[8] and that, in some cases, "the rule of expediency does not apply, in which a people, as well as an individual, must do justice, cost what it may."[9] What is often overlooked, however, is that he also criticizes utilitarian thought for failing to recognize that "it is the fault of the government itself that remedy *is* worse than the evil. *It* makes it worse."[10]

Another aspect of *Civil Disobedience* that is underexplored concerns Thoreau's misgivings about material possessions. In his view, the "rich man ... is always sold to the institution which makes him rich. Absolutely speaking, the more money, the less virtue."[11] Keeping this hostility toward wealth in mind is important because, given Thoreau's minimalist government approach, some readers may mistakenly imagine he is advocating free-market capitalism*—the dominant economic and social model of modern Western society and increasingly of many nations in Africa and Asia.

NOTES

1   Henry David Thoreau, "Resistance to Civil Government," in *Aesthetic Papers*, ed. Elizabeth Palmer Peabody (Boston: The Editor, 1849), 199–200.

2   Thoreau, "Resistance to Civil Government," 203.

3   Thoreau, "Resistance to Civil Government," 202.

4   Thoreau, "Resistance to Civil Government," 211.

5   Thoreau, "Resistance to Civil Government," 211.

6   Thoreau, "Resistance to Civil Government," 206.

7   Thoreau, "Resistance to Civil Government," 190.

8   Thoreau, "Resistance to Civil Government," 190.

9   Thoreau, "Resistance to Civil Government," 193.

10 Thoreau, "Resistance to Civil Government," 197.

11 Thoreau, "Resistance to Civil Government," 201.

MODULE 7
ACHIEVEMENT

KEY POINTS

- The concept of civil disobedience* has served as a basis for global social resistance. In this sense, it has had a universal appeal and has attracted advocates such as Martin Luther King Jr.,* Mahatma Gandhi,* and Nelson Mandela*—figures who have played key roles in the struggle for the political and legal rights of citizens of the United States, India, and South Africa, respectively.

- Thoreau explained his position on civil disobedience by using slavery in the United States and the Mexican–American War* to show how political authority can be unjust and that overcoming it can occur only through social resistance.

- Although Thoreau is normally associated with nonviolent protest, he actually argues that violence is justifiable when challenging unjust political authority—even if he was unclear about when and how it should be used.

Assessing the Argument

The immediate political problems that inspired Henry David Thoreau to write *Civil Disobedience* in 1849 were specific to the United States. However, while his attacks on slavery and the Mexican–American War were relevant mostly to the American public of his own time, his argument and conclusions are not restricted to one particular country or historical period. If anything, Thoreau's critique of the founding principles of the American political system (namely, majority rule* and the rule of law—the idea that a nation should operate according to laws rather than the autocratic decisions of leaders) has become ever

> 66 [Thoreau] is an example of the practicability of virtue, the deeply-rooted, self-cultivated individual who has the power to awaken his neighbors from their torpid lives of expediency to lives of principle. 99
>
> Michael Meyer, *Introduction to Walden and Civil Disobedience*

more relevant as more countries have adopted democratic governments.

Moreover, Thoreau's depiction of the moral dilemma in which individuals subjected to power often find themselves—the struggle that arises from the conflict between one's own conscience and the demands that government makes on its subjects—can be regarded as universal. Consequently, what he suggests as the solution to this dilemma, that "we should be men first, and subjects afterward," can also be seen as a general one.[1]

The fact that Thoreau's work has inspired people from many diverse backgrounds demonstrates its universal appeal. It was just as important for Martin Luther King Jr., a civil rights* activist and a leader of the black resistance against racial segregation in the United States in the 1950s and 1960s, as it was for Mahatma Gandhi, the leader of India's independence movement in the first half of the twentieth century, or Nelson Mandela, a black activist who was jailed for decades for his opposition to the government in South Africa and its racist policy of apartheid*—a system of deeply entrenched racial segregation.

Achievement in Context

In the twentieth century, Thoreau's concept of civil disobedience influenced countless leaders of resistance movements the world over; the most significant being Gandhi, King, and Mandela, who all used civil disobedience tactics to achieve their aims.

Gandhi developed his own philosophy called *satyagraha*, which was influenced by—but, he insisted, not based on—Thoreau's ideas. Gandhi preferred to refer to his approach as civil resistance in order to emphasize its completely nonviolent character. Similarly, King ruled out violence as a justifiable means of civil disobedience. These two, however, differ from Mandela, who initially believed in nonviolent civil resistance, but who was eventually forced to embrace armed struggle. As one commentator wrote: "When people say that Mandela 'fought' for equality, they mean it literally … He explained at his 1964 trial that [once] peaceful efforts had failed; 'only then did we decide to answer violence with violence.'"[2] For this reason, sometimes people did not consider his policy to be civil disobedience as such—but it is important to note that violence was permissible as a means to fight injustice even in Thoreau's original concept.

Although this brief list of the most important followers of Thoreau's ideas demonstrates how influential his essay was, his concept of civil disobedience contains many ambiguities. Some of them are due to Thoreau's own lack of clarity about his priorities (such as whether he favors limited government or the anarchist* preference of no government), while others can be attributed to the misreading or selective reading of his work (for instance, the understanding of "civil" as nonviolent even though Thoreau, like Mandela, admitted that bloodshed might be necessary in some cases).

Today, people widely recognize the concept of civil disobedience, yet they seem to be less aware of the man who coined the phrase than of those who have applied his principles. These tendencies and the ambiguities in Thoreau's text have led to a situation in which people understand the concept of civil disobedience in a number of different, and often conflicting, ways.

Limitations

While Thoreau made a strong case for resistance, on some points he left too much room for interpretation, making it difficult to understand exactly what he is suggesting at times. First, it is not clear when the government should be resisted. According to Thoreau, when "injustice is part of the necessary friction of the machine of government, let it go."[3] Injustice, then, needs to be sufficiently grave before one can justifiably resist authority. Again, Thoreau regards violence as permissible in fighting injustice, but he fails to specify exactly when it becomes justifiable. He seems to leave these questions to the conscience of each individual, saying, "The only obligation which I have a right to assume is to do at any time what I think right."[4]

If, however, one's conscience, which differs from person to person, is the only measure of good and bad, why did Thoreau seem to suggest that no honorable man could stand by the institution of slavery and war? Giving conscience so much importance makes his argument less narrow-mindedly moralizing—but it also makes it difficult to interpret his exact intentions or implement his suggestions.

NOTES

1   Henry David Thoreau, "Resistance to Civil Government," in *Aesthetic Papers*, ed. Elizabeth Palmer Peabody (Boston: The Editor, 1849), 190.

2   Max Fisher, "9 questions about Nelson Mandela you were too embarrassed to ask," *The Washington Post,* December 6, 2013, accessed August 12, 2015, https://www.washingtonpost.com/news/worldviews/wp/2013/12/06/9–questions-about-nelson-mandela-you-were-too-embarrassed-to-ask/.

3   Thoreau, "Resistance to Civil Government," 197.

4   Thoreau, "Resistance to Civil Government," 190.

MODULE 8
PLACE IN THE AUTHOR'S WORK

KEY POINTS

- While the political basis of *Civil Disobedience* makes it unique in Thoreau's writings, it has the same underlying Transcendentalist* core concepts as his other works.

- Although *Civil Disobedience* received little attention when it was first published, it gained popularity in the twentieth century in light of important nonviolent social movements, such as the one led by the civil rights* leader Martin Luther King Jr.*

- *Civil Disobedience* and *Walden* were Thoreau's most important works. The former explores the relationship between the individual and political authority; the latter explores the relationship between the individual and nature.

Positioning

Given that Henry David Thoreau was best known for his many works on nature, *Civil Disobedience* (1849) stands out because of its political character. But it fits into the author's wider body of work, as it was founded on the same Transcendentalist core assumptions as all his other writings. These include the belief that people at their best are independent and autonomous; that conscience is inherently good; and that conscience is the only basis on which to distinguish right from wrong. Furthermore, since most of Thoreau's works are concerned with the relationship between the individual and nature, one can regard the writing of *Civil Disobedience*, which deals with the relationship between the individual and the state, as a logical progression.

> ❝ He sympathized with the Transcendentalists' desire to move beyond the surfaces of American life—its commerce, technology, industrialism, and material progress—to a realization that these public phenomena were insignificant when compared with an individual's spiritual life. ❞
>
> Michael Meyer,* Introduction to *Walden and Civil Disobedience*

Civil Disobedience examined then-current moral theories concerning the duty of the individual to submit to governmental authority. This developed into a challenge to the English philosopher William Paley's* dominant utilitarian theory,* which saw civil resistance as illegitimate if it meant that the social harm it might cause was greater than the initial wrong it set out to resolve. Thoreau strongly disagreed, claiming that a person's moral conscience should always come before duty to the state. In cases of grave injustice, the moral thinker must withdraw support from the government, whatever the consequences.

Integration

Although *Civil Disobedience* was the first of Thoreau's early works to reach a relatively wide audience and attract a few reviews, its contemporary impact was not great, and, with the exception of the essay "A Plea for Captain John Brown" (1859), he did not pursue his political ideas in his later writings.[1]

In "A Plea for Captain John Brown"—a defense of a failed attempt to start an armed slave revolt—Thoreau reaffirms the ideas he proposed in *Civil Disobedience* about the legitimacy of violent resistance against grave injustice in. At the center of this text is John Brown,* a white American abolitionist* who fought for the ending of slavery and tried to start a slave revolt just before the American Civil War.* At the time, the press was portraying Brown's actions as foolish; Thoreau, however, expressed a great deal of admiration. He saw Brown as humane, moral, and courageous because he provoked self-reflection among those who supported slavery. Thoreau argued that those who criticized Brown did so because they were hollow and unwilling to consider the injustice of their acts. He glorified Brown for giving up his life for justice and not falling victim to material gains.

Although little known, "A Plea for Captain John Brown" is nevertheless important. In contrast, *Civil Disobedience* received considerable attention in the twentieth century after the social resistance of prominent figures such as Martin Luther King Jr.

Significance

Civil Disobedience is Thoreau's most important political work. While studying at Harvard College,* he come under the influence of Transcendentalism,* a philosophical movement that had considerable impact on contemporary American intellectual life. Strong individualism, purity of conscience, and respect for nature were Transcendentalist ideas that became important characteristics of Thoreau's writing. Readers can detect the influence of such Transcendentalist ideas throughout his work—notably in his belief that the individual and nature are inherently good but that their purity was threatened by many contemporary social changes.

Thoreau loved exploring and observing nature and most of his writings are about the natural surroundings of his hometown of Concord, Massachusetts, and his short trips beyond it.[2] Notions such as returning to nature and self-reliance are typical of Transcendentalism and important in the writing of *Walden*,[3] Thoreau's greatest and best-known contribution to the movement, in which he presents an account of a two-year experiment of simple living in a cabin that he built near Walden Pond.

While his political views had little influence in his own time, the idea of civil disobedience became increasingly important for resistance movements over the course of the twentieth century. Similarly, while his nature writings and excursion narratives only attracted modest attention at the time (with the exception of *Walden*), they are now considered to be among the most important defining works in the tradition of American literature.

NOTES

1   Henry David Thoreau, "A Plea for Captain John Brown," in *Echoes of Harper's Ferry*, ed. James Redpath (Boston: Thayer & Eldridge, 1860), 17–42.

2   Henry David Thoreau, *Excursions* (Boston: Ticknor & Fields, 1863); *The Maine Woods,* eds. Sophia E. Thoreau and William Ellery Channing (Boston: Ticknor & Fields, 1864); *Cape Cod,* eds. Sophia E. Thoreau and William Ellery Channing (Boston: Ticknor & Fields, 1865); *A Yankee in Canada, with Anti-slavery and Reform Papers,* eds. Sophia E. Thoreau and William Ellery Channing (Boston: Ticknor & Fields, 1866).

3   Henry David Thoreau, *Walden* (Boston: Ticknor & Fields, 1854).

SECTION 3
IMPACT

MODULE 9
THE FIRST RESPONSES

KEY POINTS

- *Civil Disobedience* received very little attention from scholars or the press until the twentieth century, when Thoreau's concept of civil disobedience* served as an inspiration for the social struggles of such important figures as the civil rights leader Martin Luther King Jr.*

- The most important early response to the text came from a friend and mentor of Thoreau, the poet Ralph Waldo Emerson.* Emerson criticized the author for his idea that not paying taxes is a justifiable means of challenging political authority.

- Today, the concept of civil disobedience is an important one in political philosophy. Although Thoreau's name is not often mentioned, his ideas are nevertheless central to nonviolent struggles against political authority.

Criticism

Henry David Thoreau's *Civil Disobedience* (1849) attracted little attention in its day. It appeared in an experimental Transcendentalist* periodical—*Aesthetic Papers*—that had only one issue and passed almost unnoticed by critics. Those who did review it did so negatively, perhaps because Thoreau criticized the American political system. One reviewer called it "crazy,"[1] while another, referring to a classic novel of satirical fantasy, said that "this article is as fit in a volume of 'Aesthetic Papers' as would be 'the voyage of Gulliver.'"[2]

The contemporary reviews, therefore, did not challenge the arguments that Thoreau set out in *Civil Disobedience*, but they generally

❝ He [John Brown]* was a superior man. He did not
value his bodily life in comparison with ideal things.
He did not recognize unjust human laws, but resisted
them as he was bid ... In that sense he was the most
American of us all. **❞**
Henry David Thoreau, "A Plea for Captain John Brown"

ridiculed the text and its author. The *Boston Daily Courier* wrote in a
similar fashion, "We must dismiss Mr. Thoreau with an earnest prayer
that he may become a better subject in time, or else take a trip to
France, and preach his doctrine of 'Resistance to Civil Government'
to the red republicans."[3]

The only useful comments to the ideas outlined in *Civil
Disobedience* are those that Ralph Waldo Emerson put forward.
Although a good personal friend of Thoreau and the intellectual
leader of Transcendentalism, Emerson's criticism comes as something
of a surprise, given his own works were a great source of inspiration
for Thoreau.[4]

Emerson agreed with the philosophical assumptions of the text,
with the critique of government and with the moral dilemma of the
conscientious individual whom the state requires to be, directly or
indirectly, a part of unjust social practices. He took issue, however, with
the particular form of civil disobedience that Thoreau suggested and
practiced, namely the refusal to pay taxes. Emerson called this action
"mean and skulking and in bad taste."[5] He told Thoreau that "refusing
payment of the state tax does not reach the evil so nearly as many
other methods within your reach."[6] Emerson argued that the war
against Mexico* was mainly funded by the raising of taxes on
imported and exported goods, and that if Thoreau wanted to oppose
the war, then he should find other ways of doing so.

Responses

The text did not attract any significant attention from scholars or the popular press until the twentieth century, when Thoreau's concept of civil disobedience served as the basis for the social struggles of prominent figures, including Martin Luther King Jr.

Throughout his life, the public remained indifferent at best and, at worst, hostile toward Thoreau's work. After *Civil Disobedience*, he turned away almost entirely from political topics and concentrated on nature writings[7] and on narratives of his local excursions.[8] "Although Thoreau prepared a number of his essays for posthumous publication during the last few months of his life, there is no evidence that 'Resistance to Civil Government' was among them"[9] or that he was planning to make any revisions to the text.

It is important to note, however, that toward the end of his life, and more than a decade after the original publication of *Civil Disobedience*, Thoreau did make one more reference to the idea of civil resistance. In the essay "A Plea for Captain John Brown,*"[10] he defends the soldier John Brown's raid of Harpers Ferry* in 1859, a failed attempt to start an armed slave rebellion. Here Thoreau basically upholds his previous stance on slavery, conscience, and civil disobedience with particular emphasis on the legitimacy of using violence to fight injustice if necessary.

Conflict and Consensus

The idea of civil disobedience is still influential today. Within academic circles, though, there is little agreement about the main concept and specific arguments of Thoreau's essay, and it has raised more questions than it has solved. What is clear from the voluminous literature and the lively current debates surrounding the text is that his work was highly innovative and is now more relevant than ever.

Ever since the "rediscovery" of the importance of Thoreau's essay in the first half of the twentieth century, deep intellectual discussion about civil disobedience has been undermined by the bewildering variety of interpretations and loaded meanings applied to the original concept. This multiplicity of understandings is partly due to the ambiguities of Thoreau's own writing.

Perhaps most important, he is unclear about the relationship of his theory to anarchist* thought (according to which, the very existence of government is incompatible with individual liberty). This is crucial, because he makes individual conscience the arbiter of every judgment over the legitimacy of resistance. For an anarchist, who by definition believes that all forms of political power are illegitimate, the very existence of government can be against his or her conscience. Logically then, the anarchist would regard any action directed against the state as a legitimate form of civil disobedience.

At the other extreme, some thinkers restrict the use of the term "civil disobedience" to a very narrow range of activities, notably those that are nonviolent. This may stem from a misreading of the adjective "civil." Thoreau himself openly embraced force as a permissible means of resistance against unjust governments. In short, as Edward H. Madden and Peter Hare wrote in the essay, "Reflections on Civil Disobedience," in 1970, "The results are mutually incompatible definitions all of a persuasive sort in which different groups try to put the phrase to work for *them*."[11]

NOTES

1   Robert A. Gross, "Quiet War with the State," *Yale Review* 93, no. 4 (2005): 9.

2   *Gulliver's Travels* is a fictional story by Jonathan Swift published in 1726. It was mentioned by a contemporary critic of Thoreau quoted in *Walden and Resistance to Civil Government*, ed. William Rossi (New York: W.W. Norton, 1992), 312.

3   Quoted in Thoreau, *Walden and Resistance to Civil Government*, 311. Note that this may be a sly reference to Thoreau's French origins.

4   Raymond Adams, "Thoreau's Sources for 'Resistance to Civil Government,'" *Studies in Philology* 42, no. 3 (1945): 640–53.

5   Quoted in Gross, "Quiet War with the State," 7.

6   Quoted in Gross, "Quiet War with the State," 4.

7   Henry David Thoreau, *A Week on the Concord and Merrimack Rivers* (Boston: James Munroe & Co., 1849); *Walden* (Boston: Ticknor & Fields, 1854).

8   Henry David Thoreau, *Excursions* (Boston: Ticknor & Fields, 1863); *The Maine Woods*, eds. Sophia E. Thoreau and William Ellery Channing (Boston: Ticknor & Fields, 1864); *Cape Cod*, eds. Sophia E. Thoreau and William Ellery Channing (Boston: Ticknor & Fields, 1865); *A Yankee in Canada, with Anti-slavery and Reform Papers*, eds. Sophia E. Thoreau and William Ellery Channing (Boston: Ticknor & Fields, 1866).

9   Henry David Thoreau, *Walden and Resistance to Civil Government,* ed. William Rossi (New York: W. W. Norton, 1992), 246.

10 Henry David Thoreau, "A Plea for Captain John Brown," in *Echoes of Harper's Ferry*, ed. James Redpath (Boston: Thayer & Eldridge, 1860), 17–42.

11 Edward H. Madden and Peter H. Hare, "Reflections on Civil Disobedience," *Journal of Value Inquiry* 4, no. 2 (1970): 81.

MODULE 10
THE EVOLVING DEBATE

KEY POINTS

- Today, Henry David Thoreau's concept of civil disobedience*
  is an important idea in the field of political philosophy.

- Although his views did not result in a particular school
  of thought, people usually associate them with
  scholarly literature on political obligation. One important
  contemporary scholar who built on Thoreau's ideas was the
  influential American political and moral philosopher John
  Rawls.*

- Unlike Rawls, Thoreau advocates resistance to the will of the
  majority in the case of grave injustices, supporting violence
  as a means of resistance.

Uses and Problems

While Henry David Thoreau's *Civil Disobedience* had little immediate
impact when it was written in 1849, it has proved to be highly
influential in the long term. The concept of civil disobedience has
become well known and used not only in its natural discipline of
political philosophy but also in other academic fields and the wider
public debate.

This expansion has come at a cost, however, as the concept itself
has been "stretched." So many people have applied the idea of civil
disobedience to so many situations that the term probably obscures
more than it reveals. So while the intellectual debate that Thoreau
triggered has certainly been lively, any in-depth discussion of his ideas
has been restricted to small camps, each with a separate understanding
of the term.

> **❝** Unjust laws exist; shall we be content to obey them,
> or shall we endeavor to amend them, and obey them until
> we have succeeded, or shall we transgress them at once? **❞**
>
> Henry David Thoreau, *Civil Disobedience*

One of the most important arenas of debate has been in the literature of political obligation within political philosophy. Thoreau challenged a forerunner of this debate in *Civil Disobedience*—the English philosopher William Paley.* Thoreau was going against the prevailing tide of opinion, and some remarked that the general view in this debate is inherently hostile to the idea of disobedience and that "there is always not simply a presumption in favor of obeying the law, but an intrinsic, real … duty to obey the law."[1]

Schools of Thought

While no specific school of thought has formed around the author's ideas, they clearly belong within the academic field of political philosophy. More specifically, *Civil Disobedience* directly contributes to the debate on the subject of political obligation. Arguably, the most prominent scholar who recognized and theorized about the concept of civil disobedience was the moral philosopher John Rawls in his book *A Theory of Justice* (1971), a highly influential text in contemporary political philosophy and specifically on political obligation.

Although Thoreau is often presented as a prominent American anarchist,* the relationship between *Civil Disobedience* and philosophical anarchism is more problematic than it first appears.[2] Thoreau's position on political obligation and on his ideal government was ambiguous. For example, "unlike those who call themselves no-government men," he calls for "not at once no government, but *at once* a better government"[3]—an idea to which no anarchist could subscribe. Thoreau opts for improvement in political authority rather than its wholesale rejection. As we have seen, however, he does hint that this improvement would ideally lead to no government, saying, "That government is best which governs not at all; and when men are prepared for it, that will be the kind of government which they will have."[4]

Given all of these different interpretations, it would seem that no single school has a "true" understanding of the text or adherents who can be singled out as the real followers of Thoreau's ideas. Nonetheless, the idea of civil disobedience has significantly influenced many scholars working in a variety of academic fields, in spite of their different definitions of Thoreau's original concept.

In Current Scholarship

John Rawls's *A Theory of Justice* considered when resistance to the state may be justified in "nearly just societies." For Rawls, civil disobedience was a "public, nonviolent, conscientious yet political act contrary to law usually done with the aim of bringing about a change in the law or policies of the government," and it also had to "address the sense of justice of the majority of the community."[5] He thought this was legitimate in "nearly just societies" because he believed that preventing injustice could stabilize society.

This definition is useful to highlight the most important debates and disagreements about the concept of civil disobedience and Thoreau's original intentions. Thoreau himself did not prohibit violent resistance, and he was openly critical about conforming to the will of the majority in the case of grave injustices. There is, however, still substantial disagreement about Thoreau's ideas on the aims of civil disobedience, whether such acts should be made public or kept private, and whether the disobeying subject should accept punishment willingly or not.

The American philosopher Ronald Dworkin* addressed the aims of civil disobedience by categorizing them. When the law is defied because the individual finds it immoral, he wrote, then it is justice-based disobedience. If a right has been denied to an individual, it is a case of integrity-based disobedience. Lastly, policy-based civil disobedience occurs when the law is resisted in order to change a policy that the individual finds wrong.[6]

Philosophical anarchism may not be the obvious "heir" of Thoreau's theories either, although he is often identified with this trend of thought.[7] Certainly, he makes a sweeping critique of the political obligation literature of his day in *Civil Disobedience*, even if trying to position his ideas in a philosophical framework that rejects all grounds of political power has its difficulties.[8] The Israeli political philosopher Chaim Gans* has argued that for political anarchism to be effective, it must, like Thoreau, give a central role to the duty to disobey the state when laws contradict moral values.

NOTES

1 H. J. McCloskey, "Conscientious Disobedience of the Law: Its Necessity, Justification, and Problems to Which it Gives Rise," *Philosophy and Phenomenological Research* 40, no. 4 (1980): 536.

2 Myron Simon, "Thoreau and Anarchism," *Michigan Quarterly Review* 23, no. 3 (1984): 360–84.

3 Henry David Thoreau, "Resistance to Civil Government," in *Aesthetic Papers*, ed. Elizabeth Palmer Peabody (Boston: The Editor, 1849), 190.

4 Thoreau, "Resistance to Civil Government," 189.

5 John Rawls, *A Theory of Justice* (Cambridge, MA: Harvard University Press, 1971), 364.

6 Ronald Dworkin, *A Matter of Principle* (Cambridge, MA: Harvard University Press, 1985).

7 For instance, in Emma Goldman, *Anarchism and Other Essays* (New York: Mother Earth Publishing Association, 1910).

8 Simon, "Thoreau and Anarchism," 360–84.

MODULE 11
IMPACT AND INFLUENCE TODAY

KEY POINTS

- The concept of civil disobedience* is important in political philosophy and has played a part in debates on legal theory.
- Discussions regarding the relationship between individuals and political authority date back to the ancient Greek philosopher Plato's* work *Crito*, in which we read a conversation between Plato's teacher Socrates* and Socrates' wealthy friend Crito regarding justice.
- Due to Thoreau's ambiguous explanation of civil disobedience, he has been associated with political anarchism*—a position that questions the legitimacy of political authority and argues that individuals have no obligation to obey the law.

Position

Henry David Thoreau's concept of civil disobedience has become important in debates on political obligation within political philosophy. Political philosophy and its proponents are generally hostile toward the idea of civil disobedience, and even the influential American moral philosopher John Rawls,* a leading figure in the debate, adopted only a qualified acceptance of it in certain narrowly defined cases. He certainly does not advocate refusing to pay taxes or uphold the prospect of violent resistance against political authority, as Thoreau does in *Civil Disobedience* (1849).

The concept also plays a central role within philosophical anarchism.* For instance, the political philosopher Chaim Gans* advocates a limited acceptance of political obligation. Gans suggests

> ❝ One has a moral responsibility to disobey unjust laws. ❞
> Martin Luther King Jr., "Letter from a Birmingham Jail"

that certain moral imperatives can trump the duty to obey, meaning that individuals have a duty to disobey the state when laws run counter to moral values.

In legal theory, too, the idea of civil disobedience has been an important point of contention both within and between the naturalist* and the positivist* schools. Naturalism,* broadly speaking, assesses the content of law against principles of justice and morality. Positivism* traces the validity of a law to its sources and the procedures through which it has been adopted. While Thoreau's work is not directly central to these debates, the essence of his argument is.

Interaction

Since *Crito*, a dialogue by the ancient Greek philosopher Plato, in which he portrays a conversation between his teacher Socrates and Socrates' companion Crito on the subject of justice, political thinkers have been interested in the theoretical foundations of political obligation. Why should the individual obey political authority?

Generally, political theorists have traced the basis of political obligation back to the gratitude owed to the state for the benefits that the individual has received,[1] to the duty of fair play in the cooperative scheme of society,[2] to consent,[3] or to natural duties.[4] In their quest to defend political obligation, some claim that these theories must also reject civil disobedience.[5] Many influential texts in this philosophical tradition do, however, leave room for disobeying laws on the basis of moral convictions. The political philosopher Craig Carr,* for instance, in criticizing the fair play framework, concludes that civil disobedience may be a moral necessity in certain circumstances.[6]

Philosophical anarchism* rejects all of these explanations of political obligation, arguing instead that we have *no* duty to obey the law and that political authority cannot be legitimate in the sense that it has a right to be obeyed. Although this intellectual school is probably the closest to Thoreau's thinking, given the author's own ambiguity, the relationship is not a simple one.

The Continuing Debate

In *Civil Disobedience*, Thoreau's primary intention was not to speak to a particular scholarly audience, but to encourage his fellow conscientious citizens to resist the government and refuse to support its unjust social practices. Nevertheless, as we have seen, he did openly criticize William Paley,* whose utilitarian* moral and political theories were pervasive at the time and who remained influential until the end of the nineteenth century. Recently, those working in the political obligation strand of analytic political philosophy have offered the most coherent response to Thoreau's challenge, even if their work is not directly related to Paley's thinking.

Political philosophers engaged in this academic debate consider the appropriate basis of the obligation to obey political authority. Thoreau's ideas are a direct challenge to these attempts; he argues that when political power requires its citizens to take part in grave injustices, they actually have a moral duty to disobey the government.

Civil Disobedience, then, poses an important question for political obligation theorists, and the majority of these scholars have responded by incorporating the main concept of the essay into their work, albeit in a limited form.

NOTES

1   A. D. M. Walker, "Obligations of Gratitude and Political Obligation," *Philosophy & Public Affairs* 18, no. 4 (1989): 359–64.

2   John Rawls, "Legal Obligation and the Duty of Fair Play," in *Law and Philosophy*, ed. Sidney Hook (New York: New York University Press, 1964), 3–18; George Klosko, *The Principle of Fairness and Political Obligation* (Lanham, MD: Rowman & Littlefield, 1992).

3   Peter Singer, *Democracy and Disobedience* (Oxford: Clarendon Press, 1973); A. John Simmons, "Tacit Consent and Political Obligation," *Philosophy and Public Affairs* 5, no. 3 (1976): 274–91.

4   John Rawls, *A Theory of Justice* (Cambridge, MA: Harvard University Press, 1971).

5   H. J. McCloskey, "Conscientious Disobedience of the Law: Its Necessity, Justification, and Problems to Which it Gives Rise," *Philosophy and Phenomenological Research* 40, no. 4 (1980): 536.

6   Craig Carr, "Fairness and Political Obligation," *Social Theory and Practice* 28, no. 1 (2002): 1–28.

MODULE 12
WHERE NEXT?

KEY POINTS

- *Civil Disobedience* makes an important contribution to an age-old debate regarding the relationship between individuals and political authority.
- It will probably remain relevant to this debate and to discussions on the shortcomings of the rule of law and majority rule.*
- Thoreau's concept of civil disobedience* is likely to continue to give an intellectual basis for nonviolent social resistance, as it has since the mid-twentieth century.

Potential

From the mid-twentieth century onwards, Henry David Thoreau's *Civil Disobedience* (1849) gained prominence in relation to the social struggles of important figures such as Martin Luther King Jr.,* Mahatma Gandhi,* and Nelson Mandela.* It is their names now, rather than Thoreau's own, that are central to academic debate or resistance to political authority. His core concept of civil disobedience, however, is still relevant, and his essay has been an important source of inspiration both for debates in political philosophy and for many resistance movements around the world.

Indeed, some of Thoreau's ideas have become more and more relevant over time. First, his critique of the general principles upon which the American political system is grounded has certainly become applicable to many other countries around the globe as democratic principles continue to spread. His challenges to the rule of law (broadly speaking) and majority rule (more specifically) have remained

> **❝** An individual who breaks a law that conscience tells him is unjust, and who willingly accepts the penalty of imprisonment in order to arouse the conscience of the community over its injustice, is in reality expressing the highest respect for the law. **❞**
>
> Martin Luther King Jr., "Letter from a Birmingham Jail"

important over time, and the rights of minorities have become a key theme in modern debate. In addition, his discussion of the moral dilemma of the individual whose conscience demands one thing, while the government expects another, is timeless and unrestricted by national boundaries.

Future Directions

Civil Disobedience will surely continue to be relevant to debates about the relationship between individuals, political authority, and the rule of law. It questions whether individuals must obey laws if they consider them morally unjust simply because political authority and the legal system require them to do so. In an era that sees governments implementing stricter and stricter surveillance and control mechanisms in response to popular protest, this is becoming an increasingly important question. We have seen such instances in the United States, Britain, and Spain in recent times. To take the example of Spain, a recent law was passed known as "La Ley Mordaza" (the Gag Law). This makes it illegal to take part in unauthorized protests, attempt to prevent evictions, or organize protests through social media.

Furthermore, if nonviolent protest fails to achieve more justice, can one, and should one, resort to violence to change the status quo? We have seen this question playing out in the form of riots in recent years in cities including London, Paris, and Baltimore. These are questions of the utmost relevance and unlikely to disappear anytime soon.

We can also link these questions to religion. Can someone's moral beliefs justify challenging the dominant policies backed by the rule of law? This is relevant, for example, to schooling and freedom of speech in multicultural societies.

In practice, the concept of civil disobedience can be linked to many themes of contemporary importance. These debates are not only related to Thoreau's *Civil Disobedience* but also hark back to discussions that took place in ancient Greece regarding the individual and the state.

Another issue that will probably remain relevant in the future is the topic of minority rights. Is majority rule a fair form of government, or does it result in the dominant society imposing its views on minorities? Is there an alternative system that would work better? This again is a long-standing debate that goes well beyond Thoreau's ideas. In the United States, for example, the relationship between the states and the federal government has always been at the core of political debates.

Summary

Civil Disobedience, one of Thoreau's rare political texts, asks whether the citizens of a nation have a moral duty to disobey its laws in certain circumstances. Thoreau combines a critique of contemporary American politics, and the rule of law on which it was founded, with a challenge to the ideas about political obligation that were current at the time. His conclusion was that sometimes resistance to civil government may not only be permissible but also is the only morally defensible option. Thoreau extended the ideas of his mentor and friend, Ralph Waldo Emerson,* and used the tenets of Transcendentalism,* a significant intellectual movement at the time of the text's publication that stressed individualism, simplicity, self-reflection, self-reliance, morality, and nonconformity.

In *Civil Disobedience,* Thoreau argues that every conscientious citizen has a moral duty to oppose and even break unjust laws, and he or she should refuse allegiance to a state that requires him or her to become an "agent of injustice." He gives the example of refusing to pay taxes, for which he was once imprisoned. The author applies this concept, known as civil disobedience, to the context of slavery and the Mexican–American War,* both contentious subjects at the time of the text's publication. In particular, he criticizes those who claimed to be against these developments, yet supported them in practice.

The essay challenged existing theories about government and allegiance, notably utilitarianism,* to which it proposed an alternative. Although *Civil Disobedience* received little notice at the time of publication, since the mid-twentieth century it has become highly influential and increasingly relevant, both in the academic world and beyond.

Civil Disobedience is one of Thoreau's two major literary contributions, along with *Walden,* and is his most important political text. His depiction of civil disobedience will surely continue to be pertinent to debates in political philosophy and to serve as an intellectual foundation for social resistance.

GLOSSARY

GLOSSARY OF TERMS

Abolitionism: a movement to end slavery that began in Britain in the late eighteenth century and gained increasing popularity in the United States in the early nineteenth century.

American Civil War: a war fought from 1861 to 1865 in the United States between northern (Union) and southern (Confederate) states. The issue of slavery was central to the war, since the southern states fought for the right to continue the practice.

American Revolution: a period between 1765 and 1783 when colonists in 13 of Britain's North American colonies revolted against rule from the British monarchy and founded the United States of America.

Anarchism: the belief that all government should be abolished. It advocates the free, voluntary association of individuals.

Apartheid: a system of racial discrimination and segregation in the Republic of South Africa that ended in 1994.

Capitalism: an economic system that emphasizes the private ownership of the means of production. The means of production refers to those things that are necessary for the production of goods, such as land, natural resources, and technology.

Civil Disobedience: the argument that disobeying unjust laws is morally permissible and even necessary.

Civil Rights Movement: a movement, notably active in the 1950s and 1960s, founded to advance the struggle against discrimination and secure greater equality for black people in the United States.

Concord Female Charitable Society: a charity established by women in Concord, Massachusetts, in 1814. It provided clothing and basic provisions to the needy and encouraged their moral development.

Consent Theory: a belief that political legitimacy requires the consent of the governed. The English philosopher John Locke* (1632–1704) was the first to formulate this assumption.

Foucauldian: a term referring to the philosophy of the French thinker Michel Foucault.

Harper's Ferry Raid: an attempt, led by the soldier John Brown, to start an armed slave revolt in Virginia (now West Virginia) and challenge the institution of slavery.

Harvard College: the original name of Harvard University.

Imperialism: the extension of a nation's influence by territorial acquisition or by the establishment of political and economic dominance over other nations.

Majority rule: the principle that whatever a majority of citizens decide in regards to a political issue should become the law. This is typically achieved through voting.

Mexican–American War: an armed conflict between Mexico and the United States (1846–8) that provoked tensions between the South and the North over whether the acquired territories would be free or slave states.

Missionary: a person sent on a religious mission, generally to promote Christianity in a foreign country.

Naturalism: the belief that universally applicable laws derive from ethical principles and reason.

Nonconformity: a refusal or failure to conform to a dominant rule or practice.

Poll Tax: a tax required in order to vote.

Positivism: the belief that laws must be followed even if they are unjust, ignoring moral considerations.

Slavery: the forceful subjugation of a person that strips him or her of all rights.

Transcendentalism: an important intellectual movement in the United States in the 1830s and 1840s based on a respect for nature, individualism, simplicity, self-reliance, and nonconformity.

Utilitarianism: a doctrine that argues that the correct action is one that ensures the greatest happiness for the greatest number of people.

PEOPLE MENTIONED IN THE TEXT

Amos Bronson Alcott (1799–1888) was a teacher at the Temple School in Boston and a Transcendentalist.

Aristotle (384–322 B.C.E.) was a Greek philosopher who wrote on a wide range of topics, best known for his thoughts on economics, politics, and ethics. His writing established the basis of Western philosophy.

John Brown (1800–58) was a white abolitionist* who believed that an armed struggle was necessary to overcome the institution of slavery. He led a failed uprising at Harper's Ferry in Virginia (now West Virginia) in 1859.

Craig Carr is a professor of political science at Portland State University. He is the author of several books, including *Polity: Political Culture and the Nature of Politics* (2007).

William Ellery Channing (1818–1901) was a Transcendentalist* poet.

Ronald Dworkin (1931–2013) was an American philosopher who is best known for his interpretivist approach to law. This approach stresses the importance of paying attention both to the facts and the values behind legal practices.

Ralph Waldo Emerson (1803–82) was an author, poet, and the catalyst for the development of Transcendentalism* with his book *Nature* (1836).

Michel Foucault (1926–84) was a French philosopher whose ideas about discourse (roughly, the "text" formed by a specific association of statements, assumptions, and cultural artifacts) and power remain very important today.

Margaret Fuller (1810–50) was the editor of the Transcendentalist journal, the *Dial*, and is considered to be an early feminist with her *Woman in the Nineteenth Century* (1845).

Mahatma Gandhi (1869–1948) was the leader of a peaceful Indian independence movement against British rule. He advocated civil disobedience against injustice.

Chaim Gans is a political philosopher at Tel Aviv University and author of *Philosophical Anarchism and Political Disobedience* (1992).

Thomas Hobbes (1588–1679) was an English philosopher. He is seen as a founder of Western political theory and the tradition of social contract theory. *Leviathan, or the Matter, Forme, and Power of a Commonwealth, Ecclesiasticall and Civil* (1651) is his most influential work.

Martin Luther King Jr (1929–68) was an American Baptist minister, activist, and leader of the civil rights movements. He was assassinated in 1968.

John Locke (1632–1704) was a British philosopher and leading thinker of the Enlightenment. His famous *Two Treatises of Government* (1689) and *A Letter Concerning Toleration* (1689) asserted what would become basic tenets of liberal theory.

Henry Wadsworth Longfellow (1807–82) was an American poet and professor at Harvard College (now Harvard University). He wrote many important works, including the poem, "Paul Revere's Ride" (1860).

Nelson Mandela (1918–2013) was the president of South Africa from 1994 to 1999. He was imprisoned for 27 years for his involvement in the struggle against South African apartheid.*

Michael Meyer is a professor emeritus of literature at the University of Connecticut. He is an expert on the life and work of Henry David Thoreau.

William Paley (1743–1805) was an English clergyman and philosopher best known for his work on the philosophy of religion and for his book *Natural Theology* (1802).

Theodore Parker (1810–60) was an American Transcendentalist.* He is best known for his struggle against the institution of slavery.

Elizabeth Peabody (1804–94) was an American educator and writer. She was a leading figure in the Transcendental* movement in Massachusetts.

Plato (427–347 B.C.E.) was an ancient Greek philosopher. His ideas were one of the inspirations for the modern development of the social sciences, including sociology.

John Rawls (1921–2002) was an American moral and political philosopher. A professor at Harvard University, he was the author of *A Theory of Justice* (1971) and *Political Liberalism* (1993).

Socrates (470/469—399 B.C.E.) was a classical Greek philosopher. He is widely credited as one of the founders of Western philosophy.

Sophia Thoreau (1819–76) was the younger sister of Henry David Thoreau and the editor of his writings.

WORKS CITED

WORKS CITED

Adams, Raymond. "Thoreau's Sources for 'Resistance to Civil Government.'" *Studies in Philology* 42, no. 3 (1945): 640–53.

Carr, Craig. "Fairness and Political Obligation." *Social Theory and Practice* 28, no. 1 (2002): 1–28.

Dworkin, Ronald. *A Matter of Principle*. Cambridge, MA: Harvard University Press, 1985.

Emerson, Ralph Waldo. "Antislavery Speech at Dedham, 4 July 1846." In *Emerson's Antislavery Writings*, edited by Len Gougeon and Joel Myerson. New Haven, CT: Yale University Press, 1995.

____. *Nature*. Boston: James Munroe & Company, 1836.

____."Politics." In *Essays: Second Series*. Boston: James Munroe & Company, 1844.

Foucault, Michel. *Society Must Be Defended*. Translated by David Macey. New York: Picador, 2003.

Fuller, Margaret. *Woman in the Nineteenth Century*. New York: Greeley & McElrath, 1845.

Gans, Chaim. *Philosophical Anarchism and Political Disobedience*. Cambridge: Cambridge University Press, 1992.

Goldman, Emma. *Anarchism and Other Essays*. New York: Mother Earth Publishing Association, 1910.

Gross, Robert A. "Quiet War with the State." *Yale Review* 93, no. 4 (2005): 1–17.

Harding, Walter. *A Thoreau Handbook*. New York: New York University Press, 1959.

Klosko, George. *The Principle of Fairness and Political Obligation*. Lanham, MD: Rowman & Littlefield, 1992.

Krzyzanowski, Jerzy R. "Thoreau in Russia." In *Thoreau Abroad. Twelve Bibliographical Essays*, edited by Eugene F. Timpe. Hamden, CT: Shoe String Press, 1971.

Madden, Edward H., and Peter H. Hare. "Reflections on Civil Disobedience." *Journal of Value Inquiry* 4, no. 2 (1970): 81–95.

Manning, Clarence A. "Thoreau and Tolstoy." *New England Quarterly* 16, no. 2 (1943): 234–43.

McCloskey, H. J. "Conscientious Disobedience of the Law: Its Necessity, Justification, and Problems to Which it Gives Rise." *Philosophy and Phenomenological Research* 40, no. 4 (1980): 536–57.

Paley, William. *Natural Theology*. London: Taylor & Wilks, 1802.

_____. "Of the Duty of Civil Obedience, as Stated in the Christian Scriptures." In *The Principles of Moral and Political Philosophy*. London: R. Faulder, 1785.

_____. *The Principles of Moral and Political Philosophy*. London: R. Faulder, 1785.

Plato. *Crito*. Charleston, SC: Forgotten Books, 2008.

Rawls, John. *A Theory of Justice*. Cambridge, MA: Harvard University Press, 1971.

_____. "Legal Obligation and the Duty of Fair Play." In *Law and Philosophy*, edited by Sidney Hook. New York: New York University Press, 1964.

Rosenwald, Lawrence A. "The Theory, Practice, and Influence of Thoreau's Civil Disobedience." In *A Historical Guide to Henry David Thoreau*, edited by William E. Cain. Oxford: Oxford University Press, 2000.

Simmons, A. John. "Tacit Consent and Political Obligation." *Philosophy and Public Affairs* 5, no. 3 (1976): 274–91.

Simon, Myron. "Thoreau and Anarchism." *Michigan Quarterly Review* 23, no. 3 (1984): 360–84.

Singer, Peter. *Democracy and Disobedience*. Oxford: Clarendon Press, 1973.

Thoreau, Henry David. *Cape Cod*. Edited by Sophia E. Thoreau and William Ellery Channing. Boston: Ticknor & Fields, 1865.

_____. "Civil Disobedience." In *A Yankee in Canada, with Anti-slavery and Reform Papers*, edited by Sophia E. Thoreau and William Ellery Channing. Boston: Ticknor & Fields, 1866.

_____. *Excursions*. Boston: Ticknor & Fields, 1863.

_____. "A Plea for Captain John Brown." In *Echoes of Harper's Ferry*, edited by James Redpath. Boston: Thayer & Eldridge, 1860.

_____. "Resistance to Civil Government." In *Aesthetic Papers*, edited by Elizabeth Palmer Peabody. Boston: The Editor, 1849.

_____. *The Maine Woods*. Edited by Sophia E. Thoreau and William Ellery Channing. Boston: Ticknor & Fields, 1864.

_____. *Walden*. Boston: Ticknor & Fields, 1854.

_____. *Walden* and *Civil Disobedience.* New York: Penguin American Library, 1983.

___. *Walden and Resistance to Civil Government*. Edited by William Rossi. New York: W. W. Norton, 1992.

___. *Walden; On the Duty of Civil Disobedience*. London: Bibliolis Books, 2010.

___. *A Week on the Concord and Merrimack Rivers*. Boston: James Munroe & Company, 1849.

___. *A Yankee in Canada, with Anti-slavery and Reform Papers*. Edited by Sophia E. Thoreau and William Ellery Channing. Boston: Ticknor & Fields, 1866.

Walker, A. D. M. "Obligations of Gratitude and Political Obligation." *Philosophy & Public Affairs* 18, no. 4 (1989): 359–64.

THE MACAT LIBRARY
BY DISCIPLINE

AFRICANA STUDIES

Chinua Achebe's *An Image of Africa: Racism in Conrad's Heart of Darkness*
W. E. B. Du Bois's *The Souls of Black Folk*
Zora Neale Huston's *Characteristics of Negro Expression*
Martin Luther King Jr's *Why We Can't Wait*
Toni Morrison's *Playing in the Dark: Whiteness in the American Literary Imagination*

ANTHROPOLOGY

Arjun Appadurai's *Modernity at Large: Cultural Dimensions of Globalisation*
Philippe Ariès's *Centuries of Childhood*
Franz Boas's *Race, Language and Culture*
Kim Chan & Renée Mauborgne's *Blue Ocean Strategy*
Jared Diamond's *Guns, Germs & Steel: the Fate of Human Societies*
Jared Diamond's *Collapse: How Societies Choose to Fail or Survive*
E. E. Evans-Pritchard's *Witchcraft, Oracles and Magic Among the Azande*
James Ferguson's *The Anti-Politics Machine*
Clifford Geertz's *The Interpretation of Cultures*
David Graeber's *Debt: the First 5000 Years*
Karen Ho's *Liquidated: An Ethnography of Wall Street*
Geert Hofstede's *Culture's Consequences: Comparing Values, Behaviors, Institutes and Organizations across Nations*
Claude Lévi-Strauss's *Structural Anthropology*
Jay Macleod's *Ain't No Makin' It: Aspirations and Attainment in a Low-Income Neighborhood*
Saba Mahmood's *The Politics of Piety: The Islamic Revival and the Feminist Subjec*t
Marcel Mauss's *The Gift*

BUSINESS

Jean Lave & Etienne Wenger's *Situated Learning*
Theodore Levitt's *Marketing Myopia*
Burton G. Malkiel's *A Random Walk Down Wall Street*
Douglas McGregor's *The Human Side of Enterprise*
Michael Porter's *Competitive Strategy: Creating and Sustaining Superior Performance*
John Kotter's *Leading Change*
C. K. Prahalad & Gary Hamel's *The Core Competence of the Corporation*

CRIMINOLOGY

Michelle Alexander's *The New Jim Crow: Mass Incarceration in the Age of Colorblindness*
Michael R. Gottfredson & Travis Hirschi's *A General Theory of Crime*
Richard Herrnstein & Charles A. Murray's *The Bell Curve: Intelligence and Class Structure in American Life*
Elizabeth Loftus's *Eyewitness Testimony*
Jay Macleod's *Ain't No Makin' It: Aspirations and Attainment in a Low-Income Neighborhood*
Philip Zimbardo's *The Lucifer Effect*

ECONOMICS

Janet Abu-Lughod's *Before European Hegemony*
Ha-Joon Chang's *Kicking Away the Ladder*
David Brion Davis's *The Problem of Slavery in the Age of Revolution*
Milton Friedman's *The Role of Monetary Policy*
Milton Friedman's *Capitalism and Freedom*
David Graeber's *Debt: the First 5000 Years*
Friedrich Hayek's *The Road to Serfdom*
Karen Ho's *Liquidated: An Ethnography of Wall Street*

John Maynard Keynes's *The General Theory of Employment, Interest and Money*
Charles P. Kindleberger's *Manias, Panics and Crashes*
Robert Lucas's *Why Doesn't Capital Flow from Rich to Poor Countries?*
Burton G. Malkiel's *A Random Walk Down Wall Street*
Thomas Robert Malthus's *An Essay on the Principle of Population*
Karl Marx's *Capital*
Thomas Piketty's *Capital in the Twenty-First Century*
Amartya Sen's *Development as Freedom*
Adam Smith's *The Wealth of Nations*
Nassim Nicholas Taleb's *The Black Swan: The Impact of the Highly Improbable*
Amos Tversky's & Daniel Kahneman's *Judgment under Uncertainty: Heuristics and Biases*
Mahbub Ul Haq's *Reflections on Human Development*
Max Weber's *The Protestant Ethic and the Spirit of Capitalism*

FEMINISM AND GENDER STUDIES

Judith Butler's *Gender Trouble*
Simone De Beauvoir's *The Second Sex*
Michel Foucault's *History of Sexuality*
Betty Friedan's *The Feminine Mystique*
Saba Mahmood's *The Politics of Piety: The Islamic Revival and the Feminist Subject*
Joan Wallach Scott's *Gender and the Politics of History*
Mary Wollstonecraft's *A Vindication of the Rights of Woman*
Virginia Woolf's *A Room of One's Own*

GEOGRAPHY

The Brundtland Report's *Our Common Future*
Rachel Carson's *Silent Spring*
Charles Darwin's *On the Origin of Species*
James Ferguson's *The Anti-Politics Machine*
Jane Jacobs's *The Death and Life of Great American Cities*
James Lovelock's *Gaia: A New Look at Life on Earth*
Amartya Sen's *Development as Freedom*
Mathis Wackernagel & William Rees's *Our Ecological Footprint*

HISTORY

Janet Abu-Lughod's *Before European Hegemony*
Benedict Anderson's *Imagined Communities*
Bernard Bailyn's *The Ideological Origins of the American Revolution*
Hanna Batatu's *The Old Social Classes And The Revolutionary Movements Of Iraq*
Christopher Browning's *Ordinary Men: Reserve Police Batallion 101 and the Final Solution in Poland*
Edmund Burke's *Reflections on the Revolution in France*
William Cronon's *Nature's Metropolis: Chicago And The Great West*
Alfred W. Crosby's *The Columbian Exchange*
Hamid Dabashi's *Iran: A People Interrupted*
David Brion Davis's *The Problem of Slavery in the Age of Revolution*
Nathalie Zemon Davis's *The Return of Martin Guerre*
Jared Diamond's *Guns, Germs & Steel: the Fate of Human Societies*
Frank Dikotter's *Mao's Great Famine*
John W Dower's *War Without Mercy: Race And Power In The Pacific War*
W. E. B. Du Bois's *The Souls of Black Folk*
Richard J. Evans's *In Defence of History*
Lucien Febvre's *The Problem of Unbelief in the 16th Century*
Sheila Fitzpatrick's *Everyday Stalinism*

The Macat Library By Discipline

Eric Foner's *Reconstruction: America's Unfinished Revolution, 1863-1877*
Michel Foucault's *Discipline and Punish*
Michel Foucault's *History of Sexuality*
Francis Fukuyama's *The End of History and the Last Man*
John Lewis Gaddis's *We Now Know: Rethinking Cold War History*
Ernest Gellner's *Nations and Nationalism*
Eugene Genovese's *Roll, Jordan, Roll: The World the Slaves Made*
Carlo Ginzburg's *The Night Battles*
Daniel Goldhagen's *Hitler's Willing Executioners*
Jack Goldstone's *Revolution and Rebellion in the Early Modern World*
Antonio Gramsci's *The Prison Notebooks*
Alexander Hamilton, John Jay & James Madison's *The Federalist Papers*
Christopher Hill's *The World Turned Upside Down*
Carole Hillenbrand's *The Crusades: Islamic Perspectives*
Thomas Hobbes's *Leviathan*
Eric Hobsbawm's *The Age Of Revolution*
John A. Hobson's *Imperialism: A Study*
Albert Hourani's *History of the Arab Peoples*
Samuel P. Huntington's *The Clash of Civilizations and the Remaking of World Order*
C. L. R. James's *The Black Jacobins*
Tony Judt's *Postwar: A History of Europe Since 1945*
Ernst Kantorowicz's *The King's Two Bodies: A Study in Medieval Political Theology*
Paul Kennedy's *The Rise and Fall of the Great Powers*
Ian Kershaw's *The "Hitler Myth": Image and Reality in the Third Reich*
John Maynard Keynes's *The General Theory of Employment, Interest and Money*
Charles P. Kindleberger's *Manias, Panics and Crashes*
Martin Luther King Jr's *Why We Can't Wait*
Henry Kissinger's *World Order: Reflections on the Character of Nations and the Course of History*
Thomas Kuhn's *The Structure of Scientific Revolutions*
Georges Lefebvre's *The Coming of the French Revolution*
John Locke's *Two Treatises of Government*
Niccolò Machiavelli's *The Prince*
Thomas Robert Malthus's *An Essay on the Principle of Population*
Mahmood Mamdani's *Citizen and Subject: Contemporary Africa And The Legacy Of Late Colonialism*
Karl Marx's *Capital*
Stanley Milgram's *Obedience to Authority*
John Stuart Mill's *On Liberty*
Thomas Paine's *Common Sense*
Thomas Paine's *Rights of Man*
Geoffrey Parker's *Global Crisis: War, Climate Change and Catastrophe in the Seventeenth Century*
Jonathan Riley-Smith's *The First Crusade and the Idea of Crusading*
Jean-Jacques Rousseau's *The Social Contract*
Joan Wallach Scott's *Gender and the Politics of History*
Theda Skocpol's *States and Social Revolutions*
Adam Smith's *The Wealth of Nations*
Timothy Snyder's *Bloodlands: Europe Between Hitler and Stalin*
Sun Tzu's *The Art of War*
Keith Thomas's *Religion and the Decline of Magic*
Thucydides's *The History of the Peloponnesian War*
Frederick Jackson Turner's *The Significance of the Frontier in American History*
Odd Arne Westad's *The Global Cold War: Third World Interventions And The Making Of Our Times*

LITERATURE

Chinua Achebe's *An Image of Africa: Racism in Conrad's Heart of Darkness*
Roland Barthes's *Mythologies*
Homi K. Bhabha's *The Location of Culture*
Judith Butler's *Gender Trouble*
Simone De Beauvoir's *The Second Sex*
Ferdinand De Saussure's *Course in General Linguistics*
T. S. Eliot's *The Sacred Wood: Essays on Poetry and Criticism*
Zora Neale Huston's *Characteristics of Negro Expression*
Toni Morrison's *Playing in the Dark: Whiteness in the American Literary Imagination*
Edward Said's *Orientalism*
Gayatri Chakravorty Spivak's *Can the Subaltern Speak?*
Mary Wollstonecraft's *A Vindication of the Rights of Women*
Virginia Woolf's *A Room of One's Own*

PHILOSOPHY

Elizabeth Anscombe's *Modern Moral Philosophy*
Hannah Arendt's *The Human Condition*
Aristotle's *Metaphysics*
Aristotle's *Nicomachean Ethics*
Edmund Gettier's *Is Justified True Belief Knowledge?*
Georg Wilhelm Friedrich Hegel's *Phenomenology of Spirit*
David Hume's *Dialogues Concerning Natural Religion*
David Hume's *The Enquiry for Human Understanding*
Immanuel Kant's *Religion within the Boundaries of Mere Reason*
Immanuel Kant's *Critique of Pure Reason*
Søren Kierkegaard's *The Sickness Unto Death*
Søren Kierkegaard's *Fear and Trembling*
C. S. Lewis's *The Abolition of Man*
Alasdair MacIntyre's *After Virtue*
Marcus Aurelius's *Meditations*
Friedrich Nietzsche's *On the Genealogy of Morality*
Friedrich Nietzsche's *Beyond Good and Evil*
Plato's *Republic*
Plato's *Symposium*
Jean-Jacques Rousseau's *The Social Contract*
Gilbert Ryle's *The Concept of Mind*
Baruch Spinoza's *Ethics*
Sun Tzu's *The Art of War*
Ludwig Wittgenstein's *Philosophical Investigations*

POLITICS

Benedict Anderson's *Imagined Communities*
Aristotle's *Politics*
Bernard Bailyn's *The Ideological Origins of the American Revolution*
Edmund Burke's *Reflections on the Revolution in France*
John C. Calhoun's *A Disquisition on Government*
Ha-Joon Chang's *Kicking Away the Ladder*
Hamid Dabashi's *Iran: A People Interrupted*
Hamid Dabashi's *Theology of Discontent: The Ideological Foundation of the Islamic Revolution in Iran*
Robert Dahl's *Democracy and its Critics*
Robert Dahl's *Who Governs?*
David Brion Davis's *The Problem of Slavery in the Age of Revolution*

The Macat Library By Discipline

Alexis De Tocqueville's *Democracy in America*
James Ferguson's *The Anti-Politics Machine*
Frank Dikotter's *Mao's Great Famine*
Sheila Fitzpatrick's *Everyday Stalinism*
Eric Foner's *Reconstruction: America's Unfinished Revolution, 1863-1877*
Milton Friedman's *Capitalism and Freedom*
Francis Fukuyama's *The End of History and the Last Man*
John Lewis Gaddis's *We Now Know: Rethinking Cold War History*
Ernest Gellner's *Nations and Nationalism*
David Graeber's *Debt: the First 5000 Years*
Antonio Gramsci's *The Prison Notebooks*
Alexander Hamilton, John Jay & James Madison's *The Federalist Papers*
Friedrich Hayek's *The Road to Serfdom*
Christopher Hill's *The World Turned Upside Down*
Thomas Hobbes's *Leviathan*
John A. Hobson's *Imperialism: A Study*
Samuel P. Huntington's *The Clash of Civilizations and the Remaking of World Order*
Tony Judt's *Postwar: A History of Europe Since 1945*
David C. Kang's *China Rising: Peace, Power and Order in East Asia*
Paul Kennedy's *The Rise and Fall of Great Powers*
Robert Keohane's *After Hegemony*
Martin Luther King Jr.'s *Why We Can't Wait*
Henry Kissinger's *World Order: Reflections on the Character of Nations and the Course of History*
John Locke's *Two Treatises of Government*
Niccolò Machiavelli's *The Prince*
Thomas Robert Malthus's *An Essay on the Principle of Population*
Mahmood Mamdani's *Citizen and Subject: Contemporary Africa And The Legacy Of Late Colonialism*
Karl Marx's *Capital*
John Stuart Mill's *On Liberty*
John Stuart Mill's *Utilitarianism*
Hans Morgenthau's *Politics Among Nations*
Thomas Paine's *Common Sense*
Thomas Paine's *Rights of Man*
Thomas Piketty's *Capital in the Twenty-First Century*
Robert D. Putman's *Bowling Alone*
John Rawls's *Theory of Justice*
Jean-Jacques Rousseau's *The Social Contract*
Theda Skocpol's *States and Social Revolutions*
Adam Smith's *The Wealth of Nations*
Sun Tzu's *The Art of War*
Henry David Thoreau's *Civil Disobedience*
Thucydides's *The History of the Peloponnesian War*
Kenneth Waltz's *Theory of International Politics*
Max Weber's *Politics as a Vocation*
Odd Arne Westad's *The Global Cold War: Third World Interventions And The Making Of Our Times*

POSTCOLONIAL STUDIES

Roland Barthes's *Mythologies*
Frantz Fanon's *Black Skin, White Masks*
Homi K. Bhabha's *The Location of Culture*
Gustavo Gutiérrez's *A Theology of Liberation*
Edward Said's *Orientalism*
Gayatri Chakravorty Spivak's *Can the Subaltern Speak?*

PSYCHOLOGY

Gordon Allport's *The Nature of Prejudice*
Alan Baddeley & Graham Hitch's *Aggression: A Social Learning Analysis*
Albert Bandura's *Aggression: A Social Learning Analysis*
Leon Festinger's *A Theory of Cognitive Dissonance*
Sigmund Freud's *The Interpretation of Dreams*
Betty Friedan's *The Feminine Mystique*
Michael R. Gottfredson & Travis Hirschi's *A General Theory of Crime*
Eric Hoffer's *The True Believer: Thoughts on the Nature of Mass Movements*
William James's *Principles of Psychology*
Elizabeth Loftus's *Eyewitness Testimony*
A. H. Maslow's *A Theory of Human Motivation*
Stanley Milgram's *Obedience to Authority*
Steven Pinker's *The Better Angels of Our Nature*
Oliver Sacks's *The Man Who Mistook His Wife For a Hat*
Richard Thaler & Cass Sunstein's *Nudge: Improving Decisions About Health, Wealth and Happiness*
Amos Tversky's *Judgment under Uncertainty: Heuristics and Biases*
Philip Zimbardo's *The Lucifer Effect*

SCIENCE

Rachel Carson's *Silent Spring*
William Cronon's *Nature's Metropolis: Chicago And The Great West*
Alfred W. Crosby's *The Columbian Exchange*
Charles Darwin's *On the Origin of Species*
Richard Dawkin's *The Selfish Gene*
Thomas Kuhn's *The Structure of Scientific Revolutions*
Geoffrey Parker's *Global Crisis: War, Climate Change and Catastrophe in the Seventeenth Century*
Mathis Wackernagel & William Rees's *Our Ecological Footprint*

SOCIOLOGY

Michelle Alexander's *The New Jim Crow: Mass Incarceration in the Age of Colorblindness*
Gordon Allport's *The Nature of Prejudice*
Albert Bandura's *Aggression: A Social Learning Analysis*
Hanna Batatu's *The Old Social Classes And The Revolutionary Movements Of Iraq*
Ha-Joon Chang's *Kicking Away the Ladder*
W. E. B. Du Bois's *The Souls of Black Folk*
Émile Durkheim's *On Suicide*
Frantz Fanon's *Black Skin, White Masks*
Frantz Fanon's *The Wretched of the Earth*
Eric Foner's *Reconstruction: America's Unfinished Revolution, 1863-1877*
Eugene Genovese's *Roll, Jordan, Roll: The World the Slaves Made*
Jack Goldstone's *Revolution and Rebellion in the Early Modern World*
Antonio Gramsci's *The Prison Notebooks*
Richard Herrnstein & Charles A Murray's *The Bell Curve: Intelligence and Class Structure in American Life*
Eric Hoffer's *The True Believer: Thoughts on the Nature of Mass Movements*
Jane Jacobs's *The Death and Life of Great American Cities*
Robert Lucas's *Why Doesn't Capital Flow from Rich to Poor Countries?*
Jay Macleod's *Ain't No Makin' It: Aspirations and Attainment in a Low Income Neighborhood*
Elaine May's *Homeward Bound: American Families in the Cold War Era*
Douglas McGregor's *The Human Side of Enterprise*
C. Wright Mills's *The Sociological Imagination*

The Macat Library By Discipline

Thomas Piketty's *Capital in the Twenty-First Century*
Robert D. Putman's *Bowling Alone*
David Riesman's *The Lonely Crowd: A Study of the Changing American Character*
Edward Said's *Orientalism*
Joan Wallach Scott's *Gender and the Politics of History*
Theda Skocpol's *States and Social Revolutions*
Max Weber's *The Protestant Ethic and the Spirit of Capitalism*

THEOLOGY

Augustine's *Confessions*
Benedict's *Rule of St Benedict*
Gustavo Gutiérrez's *A Theology of Liberation*
Carole Hillenbrand's *The Crusades: Islamic Perspectives*
David Hume's *Dialogues Concerning Natural Religion*
Immanuel Kant's *Religion within the Boundaries of Mere Reason*
Ernst Kantorowicz's *The King's Two Bodies: A Study in Medieval Political Theology*
Søren Kierkegaard's *The Sickness Unto Death*
C. S. Lewis's *The Abolition of Man*
Saba Mahmood's *The Politics of Piety: The Islamic Revival and the Feminist Subject*
Baruch Spinoza's *Ethics*
Keith Thomas's *Religion and the Decline of Magic*

COMING SOON

Chris Argyris's *The Individual and the Organisation*
Seyla Benhabib's *The Rights of Others*
Walter Benjamin's *The Work Of Art in the Age of Mechanical Reproduction*
John Berger's *Ways of Seeing*
Pierre Bourdieu's *Outline of a Theory of Practice*
Mary Douglas's *Purity and Danger*
Roland Dworkin's *Taking Rights Seriously*
James G. March's *Exploration and Exploitation in Organisational Learning*
Ikujiro Nonaka's *A Dynamic Theory of Organizational Knowledge Creation*
Griselda Pollock's *Vision and Difference*
Amartya Sen's *Inequality Re-Examined*
Susan Sontag's *On Photography*
Yasser Tabbaa's *The Transformation of Islamic Art*
Ludwig von Mises's *Theory of Money and Credit*

Printed in the United States
by Baker & Taylor Publisher Services